Title Page

From Colonization to Superpower: Africa's Journey to the Top

From Colonization to Superpower:
Africa's Journey to the Top

The Book, Volume 1

By: Angelo Quentin

Published By: FamilyLyfe Book Club, 2024

Introduction

The Push for Africa/Alkebulon was a period in history that saw European powers rush to colonize and exploit the resources of the African/Alkebulan continent. This era, which lasted from the late 19th century to the early 20th century, had far-reaching consequences for Africa/Alkebulon and its people. It marked the beginning of a dark chapter in African/Alkebulan history, as European nations carved up the continent without regard for its existing borders or the wishes of its inhabitants.

The driving force behind the Push for Africa was the desire for power, wealth, and resources. European powers saw Africa as a source of raw materials, labor, and markets for their goods. They also sought to expand their empires and establish colonies as a way to assert their dominance on the global stage. This led to a frenzied competition among European nations to claim as much of Africa as possible, resulting in the arbitrary division of the continent into colonies and spheres of influence.

The impact of the Push for Africa on the continent was devastating. African societies were disrupted and destroyed as European powers imposed their own systems of government, economic exploitation, and cultural domination. Indigenous peoples were subjected to forced labor, exploitation, and violence as European colonizers sought to extract as much wealth as possible from Africa's resources. The legacy of this period can still be seen today in the social, political, and economic challenges facing many African nations.

Despite the hardships and injustices of the Push for Africa, the continent is now poised to rise as a global superpower. With a rich abundance of natural resources, a young and rapidly growing population, and increasing political stability, Africa has the potential to become a major player on the world stage. As the former colonial powers of America and Europe face their own internal challenges and decline, Africa stands ready to take its place as a new center of power and influence in the 21st century.

In order for Africa to fulfill its potential as the next superpower, it is essential that its leaders and people learn from the lessons of history. The scars of colonization and exploitation must be healed, and a new vision of African unity, strength, and prosperity must be embraced. By working together, harnessing their resources, and building strong institutions, Africans can overcome the legacy of the Scramble for Africa and create a brighter future for themselves and the world. Africa's journey to the top is just beginning, and the world will be watching as the continent rises to meet its destiny.

Disclaimer, (C) Copyright & Credit

Published By: Angelo Q Kirby, and Partners 2024 1. Credit: Docular credit (unnumbered); free documents licensing warning.

9. Trade-marks: trademark ownership; third-party trademarks in books, or eBooks are prohibited from use.

10. Law and jurisdiction: governing law; jurisdiction.

11. This work may not be copied, sold, or used as content in any other manner or your name put on it until you buy sufficient legal rights to sell or distribute it as your own from us as an authorized reseller, or distributor.

12. Every effort has been made to be accurate in this publication. The publisher does not assume any responsibility for error, or omission in its or. contrary interpretations. We do our best to provide the best information on the subject, but just reading it does not guarantee success on the subject, you will need to apply every step of the process to get the results you were looking for.

13. This publication is not intended for use as a source of any legal, medical, or accounting advice. The information contained in this guy may be subject to laws in the United States, and other jurisdictions. We suggest carefully reading the necessary terms of the services/products used before applying, any activity which is, or maybe, related. We do not assume any responsibility for what you choose to do with this information. Use your own and best judgment.

14. Any perceived slight of specific people or organization, and any resemblance to characters, living, dead, or otherwise real, or fiction is purely unintentional.

15. Some examples of past results are used in this publication; they are intended to be for example purposes only and do not guarantee you will get the same results. Your results may be different from ours or others. Your results from the use of this information will depend on you, your skills, your efforts, and other different unpredictable factors.

Published By: FamilyLyfe Book Club, 2024

Title: "From Colonization to Superpower: Africa's Journey to the Top" First edition, April 2024.

Credit To:

Canva Pro: Template

Hotpot.ai: Paid Images

Chapter 1: The Colonial Legacy in Africa

Our legacy is what we make it, so we must be careful in the path that we choose in life, as it will determine how we're seen forever in history.

The Scramble for Africa

As the sun rises on the continent of Africa, casting its golden light over the vast expanse of land and sea, the echoes of history could still be heard in the whispers of the wind. The past scramble for Africa had left a deep and lasting impact on the continent, shaping its destiny and setting in motion a chain of events that would reverberate for centuries to come.

The legacy of colonization is still evident in the scars that crisscrossed the landscape, in the divisions that separated tribes and nations, in the economic inequalities that plagued the region. The exploitation of Africa's resources has enriched foreign powers while leaving the local populations impoverished and vulnerable. The wounds of the past has not yet fully healed, and the shadow of history still looms large over the present.

In the 21st century, Africa still finds itself at a crossroads, caught between the legacy of colonization and the promise of a brighter future. Global powers and multinational corporations continued to exploit the continent's rich natural resources, often at the expense of the local populations. The scramble for oil, minerals, and other commodities has led to environmental degradation, human rights abuses, and political instability in many African nations.

China, in particular, has emerged as a major player in Africa, investing heavily in infrastructure projects, resource extraction, and trade agreements which for now seems to be a beacon of hope that offers mutual benefit between the African nations and China, though there are still some concerns over Africa's long-term development. While these investments have brought much-needed capital and technological expertise to the continent, they have also raised concerns about debt sustainability, continue transparency, on the long-term impact on local economies.

Western powers, too, continued to wield influence in Africa, often through aid and development programs that comes with strings attached, which seems to continuously stunt the growth of African nations, keeping them under hostage to Western Nations, and American policies. The history of a deadly parasitic paternalism and neocolonialism relationship still looms large, as African nations struggled to assert their sovereignty and chart their own course in a globalized world.

Despite these challenges, Africa is a continent of immense potential and opportunity. Its young and rapidly growing population, its abundant natural resources, its diverse cultures and traditions all point to a future of promise and possibility. The rise of a new generation of African leaders, entrepreneurs, and innovators offers hope for a more prosperous and unified continent.

To emerge as a global superpower, Africa would need to confront its past, learn from its mistakes, and forge a new path forward. This would require bold leadership, visionary thinking, and a commitment to inclusive growth and sustainable development. It would also demand a shift in mindset, from viewing Africa as a victim of history to seeing it as a creator of its own destiny.

One key challenge facing Africa is the lack of political stability and governance. Many African nations struggled with corruption, conflict, and poor governance, which hindered economic growth, social development, and international cooperation. Building strong institutions, ensuring the rule of law independently sustainable for each country, and fostering a culture of accountability are essential steps towards a more stable and prosperous Africa.

Another challenge is the need to diversify and industrialize African economies. Too often, the continent relies on extractive industries and agriculture for its economic growth, which left it vulnerable to fluctuations in global commodity prices and limited its ability to create jobs and value-added products. Investing in infrastructure, education, and technology would be critical to shifting towards a more diversified and resilient economy.

Furthermore, Africa must engage more assertively in the global arena, forging strategic partnerships with other nations and regions, and leveraging its own strengths and resources without the fears of what America, and Western Nations think, or will possibly do to them for inserting their independent sovereignty. By working together, African nations could overcome the divisions of the past and present as a united front to the world, advocating for their own interests and priorities on the global stage.

In reflection, Africa's journey from colonization to superpower is a complex and challenging one, marked by both triumphs and setbacks. The legacy of the Scramble for Africa continues to shape the continent's present and future, but it also offers opportunities for growth, resilience, and unity. By learning from the past, embracing the present, and shaping the future, Africa could emerge as a global superpower, a beacon of hope and inspiration for generations to come.

The Global Chessboard: Balancing Influence in Africa

The geopolitics of Africa in the 21st century are increasingly complex, a myriad of global players vying for influence and power on the continent. Traditional superpowers like the United States, European Nations and Arabs, as well as rising powers like China and India, are actively engaged in shaping Africa's political, economic, and social landscape. At the heart of this global chessboard are competing interests and interactions that have profound implications for the future of African nations.

One of the key dynamics at play in Africa is the competition for access to the continent's vast natural resources. With its rich reserves of oil, minerals, and other commodities, Africa has become a strategic battleground for global powers seeking to secure access to these valuable assets. The United States and European nations, and Arabs have long-standing economic interests in Africa, with investments in sectors such as energy, infrastructure, and agriculture. China, on the other hand, has emerged as a major player in Africa, with its Belt and Road Initiative (BRI) showcasing the country's ambitious plans for infrastructure development across the continent.

China's growing presence in Africa has raised concerns among Western powers, who fear that Beijing's increasing influence may undermine democratic governance, human rights, and environmental standards in African countries. China's no-strings-attached approach to foreign aid and investment has also sparked accusations of neo-colonialism and debt trap diplomacy. However, African leaders have generally welcomed China's involvement, viewing it as an opportunity to access much-needed financing and expertise for development projects.

India, another rising power, has also been expanding its footprint in Africa in recent years. With a focus on technology, healthcare, and education, India's engagement in Africa has been more targeted and nuanced compared to China's infrastructure-driven approach. Indian companies are increasingly investing in sectors like telecommunications, pharmaceuticals, and renewable energy, offering African nations an alternative source of technology and expertise.

Amidst this web of global interests, African countries are faced with the challenge of balancing competing demands from external actors while advancing their own development agendas. Foreign aid, investment, and military presence can bring much-needed resources and infrastructure to African nations, but they also come with strings attached and potential risks. The influx of foreign capital can distort local economies and exacerbate corruption, while military interventions can destabilize fragile governments and exacerbate conflicts.

Regional actors also play a crucial role in shaping Africa's geopolitical landscape. Organizations like the African Union (AU) and regional economic communities such as the Economic Community of West African States (ECOWAS), and the Alliance of Sahel States (AES) are instrumental in promoting peace, security, and economic integration on the continent. Through initiatives like the Africa Continental Free Trade Area (AfCFTA), African nations can work towards greater economic cooperation and harmonization of trade policies to boost intra-regional commerce.

In navigating these complex relationships, African leaders must strike a delicate balance between advancing their own national interests and fostering strategic partnerships with foreign powers. They must be vigilant in protecting their sovereignty and agency, while also leveraging external resources and expertise to drive sustainable development and inclusive growth. By proactively engaging with global players and regional actors, African nations can harness the opportunities presented by foreign engagement while mitigating the risks of dependency and exploitation.

Africa's geopolitical landscape is characterized by a multiplicity of actors and interests that shape the continent's future trajectory. The intersection of power and progress in Africa requires a nuanced understanding of the complex dynamics at play and a strategic approach to navigating these relationships. By fostering sustainable and inclusive growth strategies, African nations can seize the opportunities presented by global engagement while safeguarding their sovereignty and promoting their own development agendas in the 21st century and beyond.

Impact of Colonial Rule on African Societies

The impact of colonial rule on African societies cannot be overstated. The colonization of Africa by European powers had far-reaching consequences that continue to shape the continent to this day. From the imposition of new political systems to the exploitation of natural resources, the effects of colonialism are still being felt across the continent.

One of the most significant impacts of colonial rule was the disruption of traditional African societies. European powers imposed their own systems of governance on African societies, often disregarding existing power structures and hierarchies. This led to widespread social upheaval and the erosion of traditional cultural practices.

Many African societies were forced to adapt to new ways of life, often at great cost to their cultural identity.

Another major impact of colonial rule was the economic exploitation of Africa's natural resources. European powers extracted vast amounts of wealth from the continent, often using forced labor and other exploitative practices. This exploitation left many African societies impoverished and dependent on foreign powers for their economic survival.

The legacy of this economic exploitation can still be seen in the widespread poverty and underdevelopment that continue to plague many African countries.

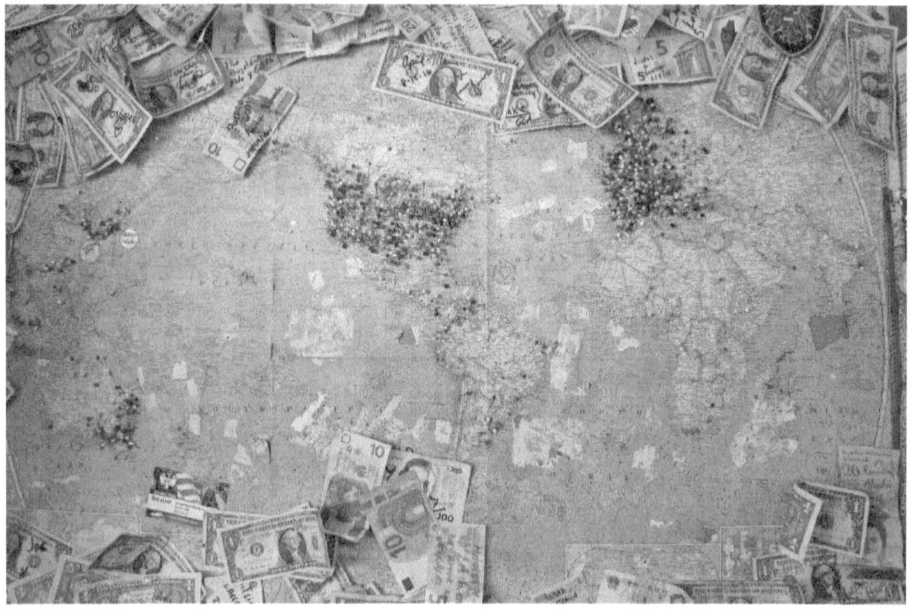

The effects of colonialism also extended to the political sphere. European powers established arbitrary borders and imposed new political systems on African societies, often exacerbating existing tensions and conflicts. This legacy of colonial rule has contributed to ongoing political instability and conflict in many parts of Africa. The struggle for self-determination and political independence continues to be a central issue for many African societies.

Despite the challenges posed by colonialism, African societies have shown remarkable resilience and determination in the face of adversity. As Africa continues its journey towards becoming a global superpower, it is important to remember the impact of colonial rule on the continent and to work towards building a more just and equitable future for all Africans. By acknowledging the legacy of colonialism and working towards addressing its lasting effects, Africa can truly fulfill its potential as the next superpower on the world stage.

Resistance and Independence Movements

Resistance and independence movements have played a crucial role in shaping the history of Africa as it transitioned from colonization to becoming a superpower. Throughout the continent, Africans have fought against oppressive colonial rule and fought for their independence, leading to the birth of many nations. These movements were fueled by a deep sense of pride and determination to reclaim their land and freedom from foreign powers.

One of the most famous resistance movements in Africa was the Mau Mau uprising in Kenya, which fought against British colonial rule in the 1950s. Led by freedom fighters such as Dedan Kimathi, the Mau Mau rebels used guerrilla tactics to wage a fierce battle against the British forces. Their struggle for independence inspired other African nations to fight against colonialism and paved the way for Kenya's eventual independence in 1963.

In South Africa, the struggle against apartheid was another key moment in Africa's journey towards independence. The African National Congress (ANC), led by figures like Nelson Mandela and Oliver Tambo, fought against the racist policies of the apartheid regime. Through acts of civil disobedience, protests, and international pressure, the ANC was able to dismantle apartheid and bring about a new era of democracy in South Africa.

These resistance movements not only led to the end of colonial rule but also led the foundation for African nations to assert their independence and sovereignty. The struggle of these brave men and women have inspired generations of Africans the fight for their rights and freedoms, and to resist from any other oppression or injustice. Their legacy continues to inspire movements for social justice and equality across the continent

As Africa rises as the next superpower, it is important to remember the sacrifices and struggles of those who fought for independence. Their courage and determination have paved the way for Africa to become a global leader in politics, economics, and culture. As online influencers and political leaders, we must continue to support and amplify the voices of those who are fighting for a better future for Africa and its people. By honoring the legacy of resistance and independence movements, we can ensure that Africa's journey to the top is one of pride, progress, and prosperity.

Chapter 2: Post- Independence Challenges

There is no fight more worthy than fighting for family, community, and country.

Neocolonialism and Political Instability

Neocolonialism, a concept coined by Ghanaian President Kwame Nkrumah in the1960s, refers to the continued dominance of Western powers over their former colonies through indirect means such as economic and political influence. Despite gaining independence from colonial rule, many African nations have found themselves caught in a web of colonialism which has perpetuated political instability and hindered their path to becoming superpowers.

One of the keyways in which neocolonialism has impacted African nations is through the manipulation of local governments by foreign powers. Western countries often exert their influence by supporting and propping up leaders who are favorable to their interests, even if it comes at the expense of the well-being of the people. This interference in domestic affairs has led to corrupt and authoritarian regimes that prioritize the interests of external powers over those of their own citizens.

A prime example of this can be seen in the case of Mobutu Sese Seko, the former dictator of Zaire (now the Democratic Republic of Congo). Mobutu was a key ally of the United States during the Cold War, receiving substantial financial and military support in exchange for allowing American interests to exploit the country's vast natural resources. His oppressive rule and looting of the country's wealth left the DRC in economic ruin, with its people suffering from poverty and violence for decades.

One of the keys in which neocolonialism has fueled political instability in Africa is through the manipulation of local governments by foreign powers. Many African leaders have been installed or propped up by outside forces in order to serve their interests, rather than those of the people they are meant to represent. This has led to corruption, human rights abuses, and a lack of accountability, all which contribute to political unrest and instability.

Additionally, neocolonialism has resulted in the exploitation of Africa's natural resources by foreign corporations, often with the complicity of corrupt local officials.

This has led to environmental degradation, economic inequality, and social unrest, all of which contribute to political instability. The lack of economic sovereignty and control over their own resources has made it difficult for African nations to develop their own industries and infrastructure, further perpetuating dependency on outside powers.

Furthermore, neocolonialism has enabled foreign corporations to exploit the abundant natural resources of African nations for their own profit, leaving the local populations impoverished and environmentally devastated. Multinational companies often engage in exploitative practices such as resource extraction without adequate compensation or consideration for the well-being of local communities. This not only perpetuates economic dependency on foreign powers but also exacerbates

social and environmental issues in the region.

Additionally, neocolonialism has resulted in the exploitation of Africa's natural resources by foreign corporations, often with the complicity of corrupt local officials.

This has led to environmental degradation, economic inequality, and social unrest, all of which contribute to political instability. The lack of economic sovereignty and

control over their own resources has made it difficult for African nations to develop their own industries and infrastructure, further perpetuating their dependence on outside powers.

For instance, the Niger Delta in Nigeria has long been a hotbed of conflict due to oil exploration by Western corporations. The local communities have faced displacement, pollution, and economic marginalization as a result of the extractive activities, leading to widespread discontent and unrest. Despite being one of the largest oil producers in Africa, Nigeria continues to struggle with poverty and inequality, highlighting the detrimental impact of neocolonial exploitation on the country's development.

Moreover, neocolonialism has led to the imposition of Western ideals and values on African societies, undermining local cultures and traditions in favor of foreign norms. This cultural imperialism has contributed to a sense of inferiority among Africans, leading to a loss of identity and a fragmentation of social cohesion. The promotion of Western consumerism and individualism has also perpetuated disparities within African societies, widening the gap between the privileged few and the marginalized many.

In South Africa, the legacy of colonialism and apartheid continues to shape societal dynamics, with racial and economic inequalities persisting despite the end of formal segregation. The promotion of Western standards of beauty, education, and success has further perpetuated internalized racism and discrimination among the population, hindering efforts to build a more inclusive and equitable society.

The economic, social, and cultural implications of neocolonialism in Africa are profound and far-reaching, affecting every aspect of life on the continent. To overcome these challenges and assert their independence and sovereignty, African nations must take proactive steps to break free from the grip of neocolonial domination.

One potential solution is for African countries to prioritize self-reliance and economic diversification, reducing their dependence on foreign aid and resource extraction. By investing in local industries, promoting entrepreneurship, and fostering innovation, African nations can build sustainable economies that benefit their own people instead of foreign interests.

Additionally, African governments must prioritize good governance, transparency, and accountability to ensure that their resources are managed responsibly and for the benefit of all citizens. By combating corruption, empowering civil society, and strengthening democratic institutions, African countries can resist external interference and promote the well-being of their populations.

Furthermore, African nations must reclaim their cultural heritage and promote a sense of pride and identity among their people. By preserving and celebrating traditional customs, languages, and practices, African societies can resist the homogenizing effects of neocolonialism and foster a sense of unity and solidarity among diverse communities. The impact of neocolonialism on African nations has been profound and detrimental, perpetuating political instability and hindering their path to becoming superpowers. Through the manipulation of local governments, the exploitation of natural resources, and the imposition of Western ideals and values, Western powers have continued to exert control over African societies in insidious ways.

To overcome these challenges and thrive as independent and prosperous nations, African countries must assert their independence and sovereignty through economic empowerment, good governance, and cultural preservation. By breaking free from the shackles of neocolonialism, Africa can realize its full potential and build a future that is truly reflective of its rich history and diverse heritage.

Economic Exploitation and Dependency

Africa has a rich history and abundant natural resources that have been exploited for centuries by foreign powers for their own economic gain. The legacy of colonization and the scramble for Africa have left lasting scars on the continent, with many African nations struggling to recover from centuries of exploitation and oppression.

The impact of economic exploitation on Africa's development cannot be understated. Throughout history, Western powers have extracted Africa's resources, exploited its labor, and manipulated its economies for their own benefit. This has left African nations dependent on foreign aid and investment to sustain their economies, perpetuating a cycle of dependency that hinders their ability to achieve true economic independence.

In the present day, globalization has further deepened Africa's economic dependency on foreign powers. Multinational corporations continue to play a significant role in controlling key industries and resources in Africa, further stifling the continent's economic growth. This unequal economic relationship has kept Africa trapped in a cycle of poverty and underdevelopment, preventing it from reaching its full potential as a superpower on the global stage.

Breaking free from dependency on foreign powers is essential for Africa to achieve economic independence and self-sufficiency. African governments must prioritize policies that promote self-sufficiency and economic empowerment for their people. This includes investing in education, infrastructure, and technology to drive sustainable growth and development.

Reducing reliance on foreign aid and fostering a culture of entrepreneurship and innovation will be key to breaking free from the cycle of exploitation and dependency. By empowering African entrepreneurs and innovators, Africa can create jobs, drive economic growth, and reduce its dependence on foreign powers.

As members of the Black community, political leaders, and online influencers, we have a crucial role to play in advocating for policies that support Africa's economic independence and self-determination. By raising awareness about the impact of economic exploitation and dependency on the continent, we can mobilize support for initiatives that empower African nations to take control of their own economic destiny.

Together, we can help pave the way for Africa to rise as the next superpower. By supporting policies that promote economic independence and self-sufficiency, we can empower Africa to break free from the chains of exploitation and build a prosperous future for generations to come. It is time for Africa to reclaim its rightful place on the global stage and pave its own path towards economic prosperity and self-sufficiency

Social and Cultural Disruptions

In the grand narrative of Africa's journey from colonization to superpower status, one cannot overlook the profound social and cultural disruptions that have shaped the continent's trajectory. These disruptions, often fueled by external forces and internal struggles, have left an indelible mark on the African psyche and have played a crucial role in shaping the continent's future.

The arrival of European powers in Africa brought about a radical transformation of African societies, with traditional cultures and belief systems being upended in favor of Western values and norms. This forced cultural assimilation had far-reaching consequences, leading to widespread social dislocation and upheaval that continues to reverberate through African societies to this day.

Furthermore, the legacy of slavery and the transatlantic slave trade has had a lasting impact on the social fabric of Africa. The forced migration of millions of Africans to the Americas and Europe not only resulted in the loss of countless lives but also led to the disruption of familial and social structures in Africa. The scars of slavery continue to haunt African communities, as they grapple with the enduring effects of this dark chapter in their history.

In addition to external disruptions, Africa has also faced internal challenges that have threatened to tear apart the social fabric of the continent. Ethnic conflicts, political instability, and economic disparities have all contributed to social divisions and unrest, creating a volatile environment that has hindered Africa's progress towards superpower status. Addressing these internal disruptions is crucial for Africa to realize its full potential and emerge as a global leader in the 21st century.

As we look towards the future, it is imperative for Africans and the Diaspora to confront these social and cultural disruptions head-on and forge a path towards unity and prosperity. By acknowledging the legacies of colonization, slavery, and internal strife, Africans can begin to heal the wounds of the past and build a more inclusive and equitable society. Only by addressing these disruptions can Africa truly fulfill its potential as the next superpower and usher in a new era of prosperity for the continent and its people.

Chapter 3: The Rise of Pan- Africanism

THOSE THAT STAND AGAINST TYRANNY WITH A JUST MINDSET WILL EVENTUALLY BECOME THE HOPE OF A NATION, CREATING A NEW PARADIGM FOR THE WORLD.

The Role of African Unity in the Fight Against Colonialism

In the fight against colonialism, African unity has played a crucial role in shaping the continent's destiny. Throughout history, colonial powers sought to divide and conquer African nations, exploiting their resources and suppressing their people. However, the concept of African and Diaspora unity emerged as a powerful force to resist this oppression and reclaim sovereignty.

African unity was instrumental in the decolonization process, as countries across the continent and the world came together to support each other's struggles for independence. From the Pan-African Congresses to the formation of the Organization of African Unity (OAU), African leaders recognized the importance of solidarity in the fight against colonialism. By working together, African nations will be able to amplify their voices on the global stage and push back against the forces of imperialism.

Today, African unity continues to be a driving force in the continent's quest for empowerment and self- determination. As Africa rises as the next superpower, the united front of African nations presents a formidable challenge to the dominance of America and Europe. By harnessing the collective strength of its diverse nations, Africa is poised to reshape the global balance of power and assert its rightful place on the world stage.

African unity was instrumental in the decolonization process, as countries across the continent and the world to came together to support each other's struggles for independence. From the Pan-African Congresses to the formation of the Organization of African Unity (OAU), African leaders recognized the importance of solidarity in the fight against colonialism.

For Blacks, politicians, and online influencers, understanding the role of African unity in the fight against colonialism is crucial. By recognizing the power of solidarity and cooperation, individuals and organizations can contribute to the ongoing struggle for African liberation and empowerment. Through advocacy, activism, and support for African-led initiatives, they can help build a more just and equitable future for the continent and its people.

As Africans continued is journey from colonization to superpower, the role of African unity will remain paramount. In the principles, cooperation, and mutual respect, African nations can overcome the legacy add colonialism and chart a new course towards prosperity and self-determination. Together, Africans and the diaspora we can build a brighter future together for themselves and future generations, reading the way towards global self-awareness, a prosperous world for themselves.

Leadership and Ideologies of Pan- Africanism

In the subchapter "Leadership and Ideologies of Pan-Africanism," we delve into the crucial role that leadership plays in advancing the ideals of Pan-Africanism. Pan-Africanism is not just a movement; it is a powerful ideology that seeks to unite people of African descent worldwide, advocate for the rights and interests of Africans, and promote African unity and solidarity. The leaders who champion this ideology play a vital role in shaping the future of Africa and its people.

One of the most prominent leaders in the history of Pan-Africanism is Kwame Nkrumah, the first President of Ghana and a staunch advocate for African unity. Nkrumah believed that the only way for Africa to achieve true independence and self-determination was through unity and solidarity among African nations. His vision and leadership laid the foundation for the Pan-African movement and inspired generations of African leaders to follow in his footsteps.

Another influential figure in the Pan- African movement is Marcus Garvey, a Jamaican-born activist and founder of the Universal Negro Improvement Association.

Garvey's message of black pride, economic empowerment, and self-reliance resonated with millions of people of African descent around the world. His leadership laid the groundwork for the modern Pan- African movement and continues to inspire black leaders and activists today.

From Colonization to Superpower: Africa's Journey to the Top

In today's world, the principles of Pan- Africanism are more relevant than ever. As Africa rises as the next superpower, it is essential for black leaders and politicians to embrace the ideologies of Pan-Africanism and work towards a united and prosperous Africa. By promoting African unity, advocating for the rights and interests of Africans, and fostering solidarity among African nations, we can ensure a brighter fulfilling life for its people.

As online influencers and advocates for Africa's rise to superpower status, it is our duty to spread awareness about the importance of Pan-Africanism and the role that leadership plays in advancing this ideology. By highlighting the achievements of past and present leaders who have championed Pan-Africanism, we can inspire the next generation of black leaders to continue the fight for African and Diaspora unity and self-determination. Together, we can build a brighter future for Africa and all its people around the world.

ACHIEVEMENTS AND FAILURES OF PAN-AFRICAN MOVEMENTS

In the quest for unity and liberation, Pan-African movements have made significant strides in shaping the political landscape of Africa. These movements have played a crucial role in advocating for the rights and dignity of black people across the continent and beyond. One of the major achievements of Pan-African movements is the establishment of the Organization of African Unity (OAU) in 1963, which later transformed into the African Union (AU) in 2002. This continental body has been instrumental in fostering cooperation among African nations and promoting the development of the continent as a whole.

Despite their achievements, Pan-African movements have also faced numerous challenges and setbacks along the way. One of the biggest failures of these movements has been the inability to fully address the issue of neocolonialism and economic exploitation on the continent. Despite efforts to promote economic independence and self-reliance, many African countries continue to struggle with high levels of poverty, corruption, and political instability. The failure to address these issues has hindered the progress of Pan-African movements in achieving their ultimate goal of a united and prosperous Africa.

Another significant achievement of Pan-African movements is the successful decolonization of African countries in the mid-20th century. Through their advocacy and activism, Pan-African leaders were able to secure independence for many African nations, paving the way for self-governance and self-determination. This marked a turning point in the history of the continent and inspired generations of Africans to fight for their rights and freedoms.

However, the legacy of colonialism continues to haunt Africa to this day, as many countries still grapple with the legacies of exploitation and oppression. Pan-African movements have struggled to address these deep-rooted issues and to create a truly united and prosperous Africa. The challenge now lies in harnessing the achievements of the past and learning from the failures to build a brighter future for the continent.

In conclusion, the achievements and failures of Pan-African movements have shaped the course of African history and continue to influence the political landscape of the continent today. As Africa rises to become the next superpower, it is crucial for black people, politicos, online influencers, and all stakeholders to reflect on the past and work towards a future of unity, prosperity, and self- determination. Only through collective action and a renewed commitment to the ideals of Pan-Africanism can Africa truly fulfill its potential and rise to the top.

Chapter 4: Africa's Economic Resurgence

Rays of hope piercing through the clouds, echoes of industry humming, forgotten streets awaken, bustling with life, Economic Resurgence Ignites, bringing the hopeless out of the darkness into the light.

Comparative Advantage

Comparative Advantage is a concept in economics that states that countries shoul specialize in producing goods and services in which have a lower opportunity cost than other countries. allows for optimal resource allocation and increases overall efficiency and productivity. In the context of African countries such as Mali, Nige Burkina Faso, Cape Verde, Botswana, Cote D'Ivoire, Congo, Chad, Ethiopia, Sene South Africa, Uganda, Ghana, Nigeria, Kenya, and Rwanda, each nation possesses own unique strengths and resources that can be leveraged for mutual benefit throu collaboration and cooperation.

For example, countries like Botswana and South Africa have thriving diamond anc mineral industries, while countries like Kenya and Rwanda have a strong agricultu base. By working together, these countries can create a regional supply chain that optimizes the extraction, production, and distribution of resources. This can lead increased trade, investment, and economic growth for all nations involved.

Additionally, countries like Nigeria and Ghana have robust oil and gas sectors, wh can provide energy resources to power industries in neighboring countries like Co D'Ivoire and Senegal.

One strategy for collaboration among these countries could be the formation of regional economic blocks or trade agreements. For instance, the East African Community (EAC) includes countries like Kenya, Rwanda, Uganda, and Tanzania, which have a shared goal of increasing economic integration and cooperation. By working together, these countries can reduce trade barriers, harmonize regulations and promote cross-border investment. This can lead to increased market access, economies of scale, and overall competitiveness in the global market.

Another strategy could involve the sharing of best practices and knowledge excha among countries. For example, Ghana has been successful in developing its cocoa industry, while Ethiopia has made strides in the coffee sector. By exchanging expe and technologies, countries can improve their production processes, increase quali standards, and expand market reach. This can lead to overall sectoral growth and diversification, benefiting all nations involved.

ırthermore, collaborative efforts in infrastructure development can enhance nnectivity and trade among countries. For instance, the East African Railway aster Plan aims to improve railway networks across the region, linking countries like enya, Uganda, Rwanda, and South Sudan. This can lower transportation costs, duce trade barriers, and promote regional economic integration. Similarly, the ans-Saharan Highway project seeks to connect countries in North and West Africa, hancing trade and investment opportunities in the region.

conclusion, Comparative Advantage offers African countries a framework for veraging their individual strengths and resources to foster collaboration and mutual owth. By working together, nations can overcome challenges, tap into new markets, d drive sustainable development. Through strategic partnerships, knowledge aring, and infrastructure investments, African nations can lead the way towards ity, progress, and prosperity on the continent.

Equal Sharing & Trading Resources System

In recent years, there has been a growing interest in exploring economic models that prioritize collaboration and resource sharing over competition and individual gain. One such model that has gained traction is the concept of an Equal Sharing & Trading Resources System, which aims to cr more equitable distribution of resources and foster mutual prosperity among countries. This syste could hold significant potential for African countries, which often struggle with economic development due to a lack of resources and infrastructure.

By leveraging their individual strengths and resources through a collaborative equal sharing and tra system, countries such as Mali, Niger, Burkina Faso, Cameroon, Cape Verde, Botswana, Cote D'Iv Congo, Chad, Ethiopia, Senegal, South Africa, Uganda, Ghana, Nigeria, Kenya, and Rwanda coul potentially unlock new opportunities for growth and development.

One of the key principles of the Equal Sharing & Trading Resources System is the idea of mutua exchange based on comparative advantage. Each country has unique resources and expertise that be leveraged to benefit other nations within the system. For example, countries like Botswana and South Africa have abundant natural resources such as diamonds and minerals, which can be trade with countries like Burkina Faso and Niger that may have expertise in agriculture or textiles. By tra these resources based on their comparative advantage, countries can maximize their economic ou and create a more sustainable and equitable trading system.

Furthermore, the Equal Sharing & Trading Resources System can also help African countries dive their economies and reduce their reliance on a few key industries. For example, countries like Nig and Ghana are heavily dependent on oil exports, which can be volatile and subject to fluctuations global prices. By engaging in trade with other countries within the system, these countries can acc new markets and opportunities that may not be available in their domestic economies. This can he stimulate economic growth and reduce the risk of economic stagnation due to a heavy reliance or industry.

Case Study: The East African Community (EAC) is a regional intergovernmental organization tha includes countries such as Kenya, Uganda, Rwanda, and Tanzania. The EAC has implemented a common market protocol that allows for the free movement of goods, services, and people withi region. This has enabled member countries to leverage their individual strengths and resources th trade and collaboration. For example, Kenya may export agricultural products to Rwanda in excha for manufactured goods, while Uganda may provide services such as tourism to Kenya in return f financial services. This has helped promote economic development and growth within the region creating new opportunities for trade and investment.

Vhile the Equal Sharing & Trading Resources System holds significant potential for African countries, nere are also challenges that need to be addressed in order to successfully implement this model. One najor challenge is the need for strong political will and cooperation among countries. In order for this ystem to work effectively, countries must be willing to collaborate and share resources for the greater ood, rather than pursuing their own individual interests. Additionally, there may be logistical hallenges such as infrastructure and transportation that need to be addressed in order to facilitate ade

nother challenge is the issue of market access and trade barriers. Many African countries face barriers trade such as tariffs, quotas, and non-tariff barriers that can hinder the free flow of goods and ervices. In order to successfully implement the Equal Sharing & Trading Resources System, countries nust work together to address these barriers and create a more open and efficient trading system. This nay require policy reforms and investment in infrastructure to improve connectivity and ensure the nooth flow of goods and services.

espite these challenges, the Equal Sharing & Trading Resources System has the potential to inspire ositive change and collaboration among African nations to achieve mutual success and development. y leveraging their individual strengths and resources, countries can create new opportunities for rowth and prosperity that may not have been possible in a traditional competitive economic model. his system can help promote economic diversification, reduce reliance on a few key industries, and eate a more sustainable and equitable trading system that benefits all countries involved.

n conclusion, the Equal Sharing & Trading Resources System could hold significant potential for frican countries such as Mali, Niger, Burkina Faso, Cameroon, Cape Verde, Botswana, Cote D'Ivoire, ongo, Chad, Ethiopia, Senegal, South Africa, Uganda, Ghana, Nigeria, Kenya, and Rwanda.

y leveraging their individual strengths and resources through collaboration and trade, countries can nlock new opportunities for growth and development, promote economic diversification, and reduce eliance on volatile industries. While there are challenges that need to be addressed, the potential enefits of this system are vast and could help inspire positive change and collaboration among frican nations to achieve shared success and prosperity.

Natural Resources and Economic Development

Natural resources play a crucial role in the economic development of any nation, and Africa is no exception. With its vast reserves of minerals, oil, and agricultural land, the continent has the potential to become a global economic powerhouse. However, the challenge lies in harnessing these resources effectively to benefit the local population and drive sustainable growth.

One of the key issues facing African countries is the exploitation of natural resources by foreign corporations, often to the detriment of local communities. This has led to widespread environmental degradation, social unrest, and economic inequality. To address these challenges, African governments must take a more proactive approach to resource management, ensuring that the benefits of extraction are shared equitably among all citizens.

At the same time, African countries must also diversify their economies beyond natural resources to ensure long-term stability and growth. This means investing in infrastructure, education, and technology to build a more resilient and competitive economy. By developing a skilled workforce and fostering innovation, African nations can attract foreign investment and create sustainable jobs for their citizens.

Moreover, the rise of renewable energy presents a unique opportunity for Africa to leapfrog traditional fossil fuel-based economies and become a leader in clean energy production. With abundant sunlight, wind, and hydropower resources, the continent has the potential to become a global hub for sustainable energy solutions. By embracing renewable energy technologies, African countries can reduce their dependence on imported fossil fuels, mitigate climate change, and create new economic opportunities for their citizens.

Africa's natural resources are a valuable asset that can drive economic development and lift millions of people out of poverty. However, this potential can only be realized through responsible management, strategic investments, and a commitment to sustainable development. By harnessing its resources wisely and diversifying its economy, Africa has the opportunity to emerge as a new global superpower, shaping the future of the continent and the world.

Technological Advancements and Innovation

In recent years, Africa has seen a surge in technological advancements and innovation that has catapulted the continent onto the global stage as a major player in the tech industry. From the development of mobile money systems to the rise of tech hubs and startups, Africa is proving to be a hotbed of innovation and creativity. This newfound focus on technology is not only changing the way Africans live and work but is also positioning the continent as a key player in the global economy.

One of the most significant technological advancements in Africa has been the development of mobile money systems, such as M-Pesa in Kenya. These systems have revolutionized the way that people conduct financial transactions, allowing for easy and secure payments using just a mobile phone. This has had a transformative impact on the economy, particularly in rural areas where access to traditional banking services is limited. As more Africans gain access to mobile money, the continent is poised to become a leader in financial technology.

In addition to mobile money, Africa has also seen a rise in tech hubs and startups that are driving innovation across the continent. These hubs, such as Nairobi's iHub and Lagos' Co- Creation Hub, provide a space for entrepreneurs and innovators to collaborate and develop new technologies. From e-commerce platforms to health tech solutions, African startups are leveraging technology to solve some of the continent's most pressing challenges. This wave of innovation is not only creating jobs and driving economic growth but is also putting Africa on the map as a hub for tech innovation.

As Africa continues to embrace technology and innovation, the continent is positioning itself as the next superpower, alongside the fall of America and Europe. With a young and tech-savvy population, Africa has the potential to lead the world in the development of cutting-edge technologies. From artificial intelligence to blockchain, African innovators are at the forefront of shaping the future of technology. As the global balance of power shifts, Africa is poised to rise as a major player in the tech industry, challenging the dominance of traditional tech giants.

In conclusion, Africa's journey to the top as a technological powerhouse is well under way. With a focus on mobile money, tech hubs, and startups, the continent is harnessing the power of technology to drive economic growth and innovation. As Africa continues to embrace technology and innovation, it is poised to become the next superpower, alongside the fall of America and Europe. The future of technology is bright in Africa, and the continent's rise as a global tech leader is inevitable.

Investment Opportunities and Trade Partnerships

Investment Opportunities and Trade Partnerships have become key pillars in Africa's journey towards becoming the next superpower, marking a shift in the continent's economic landscape. As the global balance of power continues to shift, Africa's rise as a major player in the international arena is becoming increasingly evident. With abundant natural resources, a young and dynamic workforce, and a growing consumer market, Africa presents a plethora of investment opportunities for both local and international investors.

One of the key factors driving Africa's economic growth is the increasing interest from foreign investors looking to capitalize on the continent's untapped potential. From infrastructure development to technology and renewable energy, there are numerous sectors in Africa that offer attractive investment opportunities. Countries like Nigeria, South Africa, and Kenya have emerged as major hubs for foreign direct investment, with governments implementing policies to attract investors and promote economic growth.

In addition to investment opportunities, Africa is also forging new trade partnerships with countries around the world. The African Continental Free Trade Area (AfCFTA) agreement, which came into effect in 2021, is set to create the world's largest free trade area, encompassing 54 African countries with a combined GDP of over $3 trillion. This landmark agreement is expected to boost intra-African trade and create new opportunities for businesses across the continent.

As Africa continues to position itself as a key player on the global stage, it is important for Blacks, Politico, and Online Influencers to stay informed about the latest developments in the region. By understanding the investment opportunities and trade partnerships available in Africa, individuals and organizations can capitalize on the continent's growth and contribute to its rise as the next superpower. Through strategic partnerships and collaborations, Africa has the potential to reshape the global economic landscape and pave the way for a new era of prosperity and progress.

In conclusion, Africa's journey to the top as the next superpower is well underway, with investment opportunities and trade partnerships playing a crucial role in driving the continent's economic growth. As the world looks towards Africa for new opportunities and partnerships, it is essential for Blacks, Politico, and Online Influencers to actively engage with the region and explore the potential benefits of investing in Africa. By seizing the opportunities presented by Africa's rise, individuals and organizations can contribute to the continent's transformation and play a part in shaping its future as a leading player in the global economy.

It is equally important that Africa allows the Diaspora to play a major role in the development of the continent as the diaspora only goal is not to conquer, but to build what they call home. It is essential for the Africans to understand it will never have a greater ally, then the diaspora as the Diaspora will fight until the bitter end for the mother and father land and its people.

The Diaspora is the single most deadliest weapon that the Africans have in their arsenal. The Diaspora is a ready-made army financially, mentally, spiritually, socially, and emotionally that's ready to fight for Africa against all of its enemies.

Chapter 5: Embracing Change

mbracing change, we bloom anew, transforming pain into .rength true, growth in every fall and rise, hope's wings spread, 'e reach the skies, never looking back as we choose to fly.

Emulating China's Success

China's remarkable economic growth and social development over the past few decades have been lauded as a model for other developing nations to follow. As African countries seek to accelerate their own development and bridge the gap between their current status and of developed nations, they can draw valuable lessons from China's experience. In this sub-chapter, we will explore how African leaders can emulate China's economic and social success within their own borders by implementing specific strategies and policies. We will also provide examples of successful initiatives undertaken in China and suggest how similar approaches could be adapted to the African context.

Strategies and Policies for Emulating China's Success

1. Focus on Industrialization: One of the key drivers of China's economic growth has been its focus on industrialization. African countries can emulate this success by prioritizing the development of manufacturing industries that can add value to their natural resources and create employment opportunities. This will not only boost economic growth but also help in reducing poverty and inequality.
2. Investment in Infrastructure: China has heavily invested in infrastructure projects such as roads, railways, ports, and airports, which have played a crucial role in facilitating economic development. African countries can replicate this success by investing in similar infrastructure projects to improve connectivity, reduce transportation costs, and attract foreign investment.
3. Education and Skills Development: China has made significant investments in education and skills development to build a skilled workforce that can drive innovation and productivity. African countries can follow suit by investing in education and vocational training programs to equip their youth with the necessary skills for the modern economy.
4. Promotion of Entrepreneurship: China has fostered a culture of entrepreneurship and innovation, which has led to the rapid growth of its private sector. African countries can promote entrepreneurship by providing access to finance, creating a conducive business environment, and supporting small and medium-sized enterprises.
5. Sustainable Development: China has made efforts to prioritize sustainable development and green growth to mitigate the negative impacts of industrialization on the environment. African countries can learn from China's experience and implement policies that promote sustainable development practices, such as investment in renewable energy and environmentally friendly technologies.

ccessful Initiatives in China and Their Adaptation to the African Context

1. Special Economic Zones (SEZs): China has successfully implemented SEZs, which are designated areas with preferential tax rates and regulatory policies to attract foreign investment and promote export-oriented industries. African countries can establish similar SEZs to boost industrialization, attract foreign investment, and create employment opportunities.

2. Infrastructure Development: China's Belt and Road Initiative (BRI) is a massive infrastructure development project aimed at enhancing connectivity and promoting economic cooperation across Asia, Africa, and Europe. African countries can leverage the opportunities provided by the BRI to improve infrastructure connectivity, facilitate trade, and attract investment.

3. Industrial Parks: China has established industrial parks that provide a conducive environment for manufacturing industries to operate efficiently and competitively. African countries can develop similar industrial parks to promote industrialization, create job opportunities, and boost economic growth.

4. Public-Private Partnerships (PPPs): China has successfully implemented PPPs in infrastructure development, education, healthcare, and other sectors to leverage the resources and expertise of the private sector. African countries can collaborate with the private sector through PPPs to finance and implement development projects in a cost- effective and efficient manner.

Recommendations for African Policymakers

1. Prioritize Industrialization: African policymakers should prioritize industrialization as a key driver of economic growth and job creation. They should develop policies and incentives to attract investment in manufacturing industries and promote value addition to natural resources.

2. Invest in Infrastructure: African countries should invest in infrastructure projects to improve connectivity, reduce transportation costs, and attract foreign investment. They should prioritize the development of roads, railways, ports, and airports to facilitate trade and economic development.

1. Enhance Education and Skills Development: African policymakers should invest in education and skills development to build a skilled workforce that can drive innovation and productivity. They should provide access to quality education, vocational training programs, and technical skills development.

2. Promote Entrepreneurship: African countries should promote entrepreneurship by providing access to finance, creating a conducive business environment, and supporting small and medium-sized enterprises. They should encourage innovation and creativity to drive economic growth and job creation.

3. Prioritize Sustainable Development: African policymakers should prioritize sustainable development practices to mitigate the negative impacts of industrialization on the environment. They should invest in renewable energy, promote green growth, and adopt environmentally friendly technologies.

Conclusion

In conclusion, African leaders can emulate China's economic and social success by implementing specific strategies and policies that focus on industrialization, infrastructure development, education and skills development, entrepreneurship, and sustainable development. By drawing lessons from China's experience and adapting successful initiatives to the African context, policymakers can accelerate economic growth, reduce poverty, and promote social development. It is imperative for African countries to prioritize these key areas to bridge the development gap and achieve sustainable and inclusive growth.

AFRICA FIRST AND THE WORLD LAST

I propose a set of economic policies aimed at revolutionizing the way African nations manage and monetize their natural resources. These policies suggest that each country should establish state-owned conglomerates to oversee their natural resources, prioritize intra-African trade, and set up intercontinental banking centers. Additionally, I advocate for African countries to focus on selling a single product base to the continent and to assert their rights to nationalize claims and protect their resources.

The idea of each African country establishing state-owned conglomerates for their natural resources is an interesting one. By having the government take control of these resources, it could ensure that they are managed efficiently and fairly. This could potentially lead to greater transparency and accountability in the management of these valuable assets.

However, there may be challenges in implementing such a system, such as concerns about government corruption and inefficiency. Additionally, there may be resistance from international companies that currently have stakes in these resources.

Prioritizing intra-African trade is another key component of the proposed economic policies. By encouraging African nations to trade among themselves first, it could help to boost regional economic growth and integration. This could lead to increased economic cooperation and stability within the continent. However, there may be challenges in terms of infrastructure and logistics, as well as differences in trade regulations and standards among African countries.

Setting up intercontinental banking centers in gold-rich African countries could have significant benefits for the continent. It could attract investment and promote economic development by becoming financial hubs for the region. This could help to strengthen Africa's position in the global economy and enhance its financial independence. However, there may be challenges in terms of building the necessary infrastructure and expertise to establish such centers. There may also be concerns about the potential for these centers to become magnets for illicit financial activities.

Focusing on selling a single product base to the entire continent could help African countries to specialize and maximize their resources. By concentrating on one product, they could become more competitive in the global market and generate greater revenues. This could help to diversify their economies and reduce dependence on volatile commodity prices. However, there may be risks in terms of overreliance on a single product and vulnerability to market fluctuations.

The concept of African nations claiming and protecting their resources as a means of development and empowerment is a powerful one. It reflects the idea that African countries have the right to assert their sovereignty over their own resources and use them for the benefit of their people. This could help to address historical injustices and promote economic self-sufficiency. However, there may be challenges in terms of legal frameworks and enforcement mechanisms to protect these resources from exploitation.

There are examples of countries that have successfully implemented similar strategies to the ones proposed in my book. For instance, Norway has established a state-owned oil company, Equinor, to manage its oil resources. This has allowed Norway to efficiently regulate its oil industry and generate significant revenues for the government. Likewise, Singapore has developed into a major financial center by attracting foreign investment and promoting economic growth. These examples demonstrate the potential benefits of state-led resource management and financial development.

However, there are also potential challenges and criticisms of the proposed policies. Critics may argue that state-owned conglomerates could be prone to corruption and mismanagement, leading to inefficiencies and losses. There may also be concerns about the impact of prioritizing intra-African trade on trade relations with other regions. Additionally, setting up intercontinental banking centers could face opposition from established financial centers that may view them as competitors.

My book Offers a bold vision for transforming the way African nations manage and monetize their natural resources. By establishing state-owned conglomerates, prioritizing intra-African trade, and setting up intercontinental banking centers, African countries could enhance their economic growth and assert their sovereignty over their resources. While there may be challenges in implementing these policies, they hold the potential to empower African nations and promote sustainable development on the continent.

OW THE CHINESE ECONOMY SYSTEM WORKS

The Chinese economy is a unique blend of socialism and capitalism, often referred to as a hybrid socialist- capitalist system. This system has evolved significantly since China began its economic reforms in the late1970s under Deng Xiaoping. The Chinese economy is characterized by a strong central government that sets economic goals and policies, while also allowing for a market-oriented approach to production and distribution.

Comparing the Chinese economy to the pure socialist system of the former Soviet Union, we can see significant differences in terms of centralization and decentralization. In the Soviet Union, the economy was highly centralized, with the government controlling all means of production and distribution. This led to inefficiencies and a lack of innovation, ultimately contributing to the collapse of the Soviet Union in1991.

In contrast, the Chinese economy has embraced some level of decentralization, allowing for greater flexibility and adaptation to market forces. While the Chinese government maintains a strong presence in key industries such as banking, energy, and telecommunications, there is also a significant degree of autonomy at the provincial and local levels. This balance between centralization and decentralization has allowed China to achieve rapid economic growth while also adapting to changing global economic conditions.

To understand the hierarchical structure of the Chinese economy, we can draw parallels to a corporation. At the top of the hierarchy are the independent owners, and in some cases the Chinese government and Communist Party. The government sets economic goals and policies, while the party ensures adherence to socialist principles. Below the owners are the executives, who oversee the implementation of policies and manage key industries and sectors. Not all but close to 20% of these executives are often high- ranking government officials who have significant influence over economic decision-making

Managers in the Chinese economy play a crucial role in coordinating production and distribution, ensuring that resources are allocated efficiently and according to government guidelines. These managers have a high level of autonomy within their departments, allowing for innovation and adaptation to market conditions. Finally, employees in the Chinese economy are the workers who carry out the day-to- day operations of businesses and industries. While workers have some input in decision-making through worker councils, ultimately the government retains final authority.

One strength of the hierarchical structure of the Chinese economy is that it allows for clear direction and coordination of economic activities. The government can set strategic goals and priorities, which are then implemented through the various levels of the hierarchy. This top-down approach has been instrumental in China's economic development, enabling the country to achieve rapid industrialization and urbanization.

However, one weakness of this hierarchical structure is that it can lead to inefficiencies and bureaucracy. Decisions often have to pass through multiple layers of government before being implemented, which can slow down the pace of economic reform and adaptation. Additionally, the lack of transparency and accountability in the Chinese economy can lead to corruption and favoritism, undermining the overall effectiveness of the system.

In comparison to the capitalist system of America, the Chinese economy is more centralized and government-directed. While the American economy is driven by market forces and individual entrepreneurship, the Chinese economy is guided by government policies and long-term planning.

This difference in approach has led to significant disparities in economic development and wealth distribution between the two countries. Overall, the Chinese economy system is a complex blend of socialism and capitalism, with a hierarchical structure that resembles a corporation. By balancing centralization and decentralization,

China has been able to achieve rapid economic growth while also maintaining political stability. However, the system is not without its challenges, including inefficiencies and corruption. As China continues to navigate its path towards economic reform, it will be crucial to strike the right balance between government control and market forces.

Power Points:

1. The Chinese economy can be seen a hybrid system, combining of socialism and capitalism create a unique economic model.

2. The hierarchical structure of the Chinese economy resembles that of a corporation, with owners, executives, managers, and employees.
3. Employees work under managers, who report to executives, who in turn answer to the owners, demonstrating a top-down authority system.
4. Despite the centralized nature of the Chinese economy, there is also a level of autonomy within departments for some independence in decision-making.
5. This balance between centralization and decentralization sets the Chinese economic system apart from the pure socialist system seen in the former Soviet Union and the more capitalist system in the United States.
6. The Chinese economy has demonstrated success in balancing these competing economic ideologies, driving strong economic growth and development over the past few decades.
7. The government plays a significant role in the Chinese economy, guiding and directing economic activities to achieve specific goals and outcomes.
8. China's state-owned enterprises (SOEs) play a crucial role in the economy, with the government exerting control over key industries and sectors.
9. The Chinese economy's emphasis on long-term planning and strategic decision- making has enabled it to navigate global economic challenges and maintain steady growth.
10. The Chinese economy's unique blend of socialist and capitalist elements has positioned it as a formidable player in the global economy, with significant influence and impact on international trade and investment.

Africa Economic Instruction Protectionism

China's economic instruction protectionism policies have played a pivotal role in the country technological sovereignty and industrial advancement. By requiring joint partnerships and local equity stakes for foreign firms investing in China, as well as promoting voluntary technology transfer, along with requiring all foreign firms like Amazon to partner with local Chinese firms and often to have equity owned by Chinese investors so they're partially Chinese companies defending its economic sovereignty.

China has been able to move up the supply chain of production and become a major player in global manufacturing. These policies have not only strengthened China's economic position but have also allowed the country to avoid the pitfalls of traditional forms of colonization by ensuring that foreign companies contribute to the country's economic development and technological advancement. African leaders also need to think not just about physical colonization but also about economic colonization, technological colonization, digital colonization, software colonization, industrial colonization, and land colonization.

One of the keys of China's economic instruction protectionism policies is the requirement for joint partnerships and local equity stakes for foreign firms investing in the country. This ensures that foreign companies are not simply exploiting China's resources and labor force for their own benefit but are also contributing to the growth of local industries and technology capabilities. By forging partnerships with local firms and having Chinese investors hold equity in their operations, foreign companies are incentivized to transfer technology and knowledge to their Chinese counterparts, thus helping to build domestic technological capabilities.

China has fostered these strategies where they don't simply just welcome in all foreign direct investment without any conditions, I mean they have pondered modern strategy in a manner that has made them all the more technologically sovereign. This has helped China assist in fostering the supply chain at every level and now China isn't just dependent on foreign corporations to simply survive economically but also to advance technologically.

With good geopolitical economy policies, like for instance the Chinese government required foreign firms that were investing in China to have joint partnerships with local firms and to have local equity ownership, China also required technology transfer for foreign companies that invested in China wanting to get access to cheap labor.

Additionally, China's emphasis on voluntary technology transfer has been a crucial factor in its development as a global manufacturing powerhouse. Rather than forcing foreign companies to share their technology, China has encouraged technology transfer through mutually beneficial partnerships. This approach has allowed Chinese companies to gain access to advanced technologies and processes, leading to rapid innovation and growth in key industries such as electronics, telecommunications, and automotive manufacturing. By leveraging the expertise of foreign firms while also fostering local innovation, China has been able to position itself as a leader in technological development and industrial production.

Furthermore, China's focus on economic sovereignty in key sectors such as telecommunications, construction, transportation, and banking has enabled the country to maintain control over critical infrastructure and services. State-owned enterprises dominate these sectors, ensuring that they are operated in the best interests of the Chinese people rather than for private profit. This approach has not only safeguarded essential services but has also facilitated strategic investments in infrastructure development, transportation networks, and financial systems, all of which are essential for sustained economic growth.

In contrast to traditional forms of colonization, which often involved the exploitation and extraction of resources for the benefit of foreign powers, China's economic instruction protectionism policies prioritize mutual cooperation and shared benefits. By requiring foreign companies to contribute to the

local economy through joint ventures and technology transfer, China has been able to foster long-term partnerships that support its industrial advancement and technological sovereignty. This approach has not only benefited China but has also created opportunities for other developing countries, including those in Africa, to learn from China's experiences and adopt similar policies to enhance their own economic development

For Africa, adopting similar economic instruction protectionism policies could provide numerous benefits in terms of industrial advancement and technological sovereignty. By requiring joint partnerships

and local equity stakes for foreign firms investing in the region, African countries can ensure that foreign investment contributes to local economic development and technology transfer. This will help to build domestic capabilities, create employment opportunities, and stimulate innovation in key industries, ultimately leading to sustainable economic growth and prosperity.

Moreover, promoting voluntary technology transfer and emphasizing economic sovereignty in strategic sectors can help African countries to avoid the pitfalls of economic colonization and ensure that they retain control over critical infrastructure and services. By learning from China's experiences and implementing similar policies, African countries can position themselves as key players in the global economy and accelerate their development as industrial and technological hubs.

In conclusion, China's economic instruction protectionism policies have been instrumental in the country's technological sovereignty and industrial advancement. By requiring joint partnerships, local equity stakes, and technology transfer for foreign firms investing in China, the country has been able to move up the supply chain of production and become a global manufacturing powerhouse. These policies have not only strengthened China's economic position but have also allowed the country to maintain control over key industries and infrastructure. By adopting similar policies, African countries can enhance their own economic development and technological capabilities, ultimately leading to prosperity and competitiveness in the global market.

tate Ownership

In addition, implementing lease land laws for foreign companies with limitations on ownership duration can prevent exploitation and ensure that the country benefits from the resources extracted. By allowing only a percentage of profits to be shared with foreign companies, African countries can protect their wealth and natural resources from being plundered by multinational corporations.

State ownership of mineral mines is another important aspect that can safeguard national interests. By ensuring that these resources are controlled by the government, African nations can regulate the extraction process, prevent environmental degradation, and ensure that the profits generated benefit the local population

All mineral mines should be state owned so that foreigners can't come into the country and steal the country's wealth. This law should also apply to oil reserves and anything of high value extracted from the Earth. Foreign companies shouldn't be allowed to build a refinery or plants to extract any resource without paying leasing license, also only allow 30% of the profits with 70% going to the state, again, they must align themselves with a partner that's native to that country or a diaspora living in that country.

Profit-sharing regulations with foreign companies can also be implemented to ensure that the wealth generated from these resources is distributed equitably. By establishing partnerships with local stakeholders, such as diaspora communities or native residents, foreign companies can contribute to the economic development of the country while respecting local interests and maintaining sovereignty.

Overall, African and Diaspora Land Settlements Laws are essential for protecting the rights of the people, preserving sovereignty, and promoting sustainable development. By adopting regulations similar to those in the Philippines and other successful countries, African nations can safeguard their resources, prevent exploitation, and empower local communities to benefit from their land and natural wealth.

Chapter 6: What Africa Needs To Be Sovereign Countries

Shackles shattered, now voices will rise, from the past to new sunrise, sovereign souls demand their right, as Africannations shine with might, swearin never again to lose their light.

Multiple Industrial Parks

Establishing multiple industrial parks in each country across Africa will significantly impact economic development, job creation, and advancement across various sectors. By focusing on sectors like Clothing, Woodworking, Metalworking, Cell Phone Creation, Building Local Transportation, Building Public Transportation, Computers, Televisions, Software, and Military Hardware, African countries can diversify their economies, attract investment, and create sustainable opportunities.

Clothing manufacturing can stimulate economic growth by creating jobs, boosting exports, and reducing reliance on imported goods. Woodworking and metalworking industries can capitalize on Africa's rich natural resources to produce-quality furniture, construction materials, and machinery. Cell phone creation and technology manufacturing can drive innovation and enhance connectivity within the continent. Building local and public transportation infrastructure can improve mobility, accessibility, and efficiency for urban populations. Investing in computers, televisions, software development, and military hardware can promote technological advancement, national security, and competitiveness in the global market.

Each sector presents unique benefits and challenges in terms of workforce development. Clothing manufacturing, woodworking, and metalworking industries offer opportunities for low-skilled workers to access stable employment and acquire valuable technical skills. Cell phone creation, technology manufacturing, and software development require a highly skilled workforce with expertise in engineering, design, and programming. Building transportation infrastructure demands labor-intensive construction work, project management, and logistics expertise. Military hardware production entails specialized training, security clearance, and compliance with international regulations.

The proposed workforce structure should consider different wage rates, work hours, and employment arrangements based on the skill level, experience, and industry requirements. Low-skilled workers in clothing manufacturing, woodworking, and metalworking industries may receive minimum wages, work in shifts, and engage in piece-rate production.

Double & Quadruple Your Workforce: Weekday Group 1: 10 hours a day, $5.50 an hour minimum wage, pay biweekly working, four days a week =$440. Weekend Group 2: 10 hours a day, $5.50 an hour minimum wage, paid biweekly, working three days a week =$330.

In some cases, you could hire a night shift. Nightshift Group 3: 10 hours a day, $5.50 an hour minimum wage, pay biweekly, work four days a week =$440. Weekend Nightshift Group 4: 10 hours a day, $5.50 an hour minimum wage, paid biweekly, working three days a week =$330.

Under the same circumstances, which would quadruple the workforce at one job, as each work group will be a separate entity. By doing it this way, instead of having 100 people working in a healthy environment, it becomes 400 people working in a healthy environment.

Highly skilled workers in technology, software development, and military hardware sectors may receive competitive salaries, work flexible hours, and participate in innovation projects. Construction workers in transportation infrastructure projects may earn hourly wages, work overtime, and have access to safety training programs.

Quadrupling the workforce through this model can improve productivity, generate revenue, and accelerate economic growth. However, it is essential to prioritize labor rights, employee well-being, and sustainable development practices. Protecting workers' rights, ensuring fair wages, providing adequate benefits, and promoting a safe working environment are crucial for long-term prosperity. Strengthening labor regulations, enforcing ethical standards, and investing in social programs can enhance workforce management and promote inclusive growth.

To optimize workforce management and ensure a successful transition to a more industrialized economy in Africa, policymakers and stakeholders should focus on the following recommendations:

1. Invest in education and training programs to develop a skilled workforce for emergi industries.
2. Implement policies to promote gender equality, diversity, and inclusivity in the workplace.
3. Support small and medium-sized enterprises (SMEs) to foster

entrepreneurship, innovation, and local production.

4. Establish public-private partnerships to leverage resources, expertise, and technolog transfer for

industrial development.

5. Enhance infrastructure, logistics, and connectivity to facilitate trade, investment, anc market access.

By strategically developing multiple industrial parks across Africa and leveraging th potential of key sectors like Clothing, Woodworking, Metalworking, Cell Phone Creation, Building Local Transportation, Building Public Transportation, Comput Televisions, Software, and Military Hardware, African countries can harness their economic potential, create sustainable jobs, and achieve technological advancemen for a brighter future.

The Establishment of Multiple Agricultural Parks

Africa has long been seen as the sleeping giant of global economic power due to its abundant natural resources and fertile lands. However, for the continent to truly realize its potential, it must focus on revolutionizing its agricultural sector. One key strategy that holds promise in this regard is the establishment of Multiple Agricultural Parks (MAPs) across Africa.

MAPs are designated areas where farmers are provided with land, equipment, and access to markets to increase productivity and profitability. These parks serve as hubs for agricultural innovation, bringing together farmers, researchers, and experts to collaborate and share best practices. By providing farmers with the resources, they need to succeed, MAPs have the potential to drive economic development and promote self-reliance across the continent. The governments of these agricultural parks will provide land and equipment for farmers to produce various crops, including domestic crops like corn, cotton, wheat, and grains, as well as rice crops for export markets.

One of the key benefits of MAPs is the ability to boost agricultural productivity. Research has shown that providing farmers with the necessary tools and resources can significantly increase crop yields. This not only benefits individual farmers, but also has a ripple effect on the economy. Increased agricultural productivity leads to higher incomes for farmers, which in turn stimulates demand for goods and services, creating a multiplier effect that spurs overall economic growth.

Moreover, MAPs can play a crucial role in promoting food security in Africa. By providing farmers with access to markets, these parks help ensure a stable food supply for each country and the continent. This not only reduces the risk of famine and hunger, but also strengthens Africa's position in the global food market. With a reliable food supply, African countries can better negotiate trade agreements and become key players in the international arena.

Real-life examples from countries like India, China, and Brazil demonstrate the power of agricultural parks in driving economic development. In China, for instance, the establishment of agricultural parks has led to a dramatic increase in food production, turning the country from a net food importer to a net food exporter. Similarly, Brazil has utilized agricultural parks to boost its agricultural sector, turning the country into a global agricultural powerhouse.

In order for Africa to replicate this success, it must prioritize the establishment of Multiple Agricultural Parks across the continent. This model can be implemented effectively by leveraging existing infrastructure and resources. By providing farmers with the tools, they need to thrive, MAPs have the potential to transform Africa's agricultural sector and propel the continent towards becoming a superpower.

In conclusion, the establishment of Multiple Agricultural Parks in Africa holds immense potential in driving economic development, promoting self-reliance, and ensuring food security across the continent. By providing farmers with land, equipment, and access to markets, MAPs can unleash the full potential of Africa's agricultural sector and pave the way for the continent to become a global economic powerhouse. It is time for African leaders to prioritize the development of MAPs and unlock the transformative power of agriculture in Africa's journey towards prosperity.

Hi Tech Schools & Trade Schools

Hi-Tech Schools will play a crucial role in preparing Africa's youth for success in the digital economy by offering comprehensive training in a range of-demand engineering discipline. Engineering is a critical field that drives innovation, development, and growth in the modern world. Africa's future as a global superpower rests on its ability to produce skilled engineers who can design, build, and maintain the advanced technologies needed to compete on the global stage.

Semiconductor engineering, for example, is a key area in which Africa has the potential to excel. Semiconductors are the building blocks of modern electronics, and a solid foundation in this field can pave the way for Africa to become a hub for technological innovation. By training students in semiconductor engineering, Hi-Tech Schools are helping to bridge the gap between Africa's current technological capabilities and the demands of the fast-evolving global tech industry.

Similarly, military hardware engineering plays a critical role in Africa's development, given the continent's complex security challenges. By equipping students with the skills needed to design and manufacture advanced military equipment, Hi-Tech Schools are contributing to Africa's security and defense capabilities, while also creating new opportunities for growth and innovation.

Software engineering, cyber engineering, and technical engineering are also key focus areas for Hi-Tech Schools, as they prepare students for careers in the rapidly expanding fields of software development, cybersecurity, and technical specialization. By providing hands-on training and real-world experience, these schools are enabling students to develop practical skills that are directly applicable to the digital economy.

On the other hand, Trade Schools are playing a vital role in addressing the needs of local industries and empowering individuals economically through vocational education. Nursing, for example, is a critical sector that requires skilled professionals to provide quality healthcare services to communities across Africa. By offering training in nursing, Trade Schools are contributing to the overall health and well-being of the population, while also creating new job opportunities for individuals seeking a rewarding and fulfilling career in healthcare.

Agricultural farming is another key area in which Trade Schools are making a difference. Agriculture should always be the backbone of every African economy, and by training individuals in agricultural farming techniques, Trade Schools are helping to increase productivity, reduce food insecurity, and improve livelihoods for farmers and their families. By equipping individuals with the skills needed to grow and harvest crops sustainably, Trade Schools are contributing to the long-term prosperity of African communities.

In addition to nursing and agricultural farming, Trade Schools also offer training in masonry, plumbing, electrical work, carpentry, and metalworking. These essential skills are in high demand across a wide range of industries, and by providing vocational education in these areas, Trade Schools are helping to address the skills gap and create new opportunities for individuals to secure stable and well-paying jobs.

The impact of these educational initiatives on Africa's journey towards becoming a global superpower cannot be overstated. By investing in both Hi-Tech Schools and Trade Schools, African countries are laying the foundation for sustainable development, economic growth, and prosperity for all. With a skilled workforce equipped with the knowledge and skills needed to drive innovation, create new industries, and improve the quality of life for all citizens, Africa is well-positioned to take its place on the global stage as a leader in technology, industry, and innovation.

The impact of Hi-Tech Schools and Trade Schools on Africa's journey towards becoming a global superpower is profound. By offering comprehensive training in high-demand engineering disciplines and essential vocational skills, these schools are preparing a new generation of innovators, entrepreneurs, and skilled professionals who can drive growth and prosperity in the region. With a focus on agriculture, infrastructure development, and human capital development, African countries are on track to achieve sustainable development and a brighter future for generations to come. Through investment in education, training, and skills development, Africa is poised to emerge as a global leader in technology, industry, and innovation, setting an example for the rest of the world to follow.

Basic Public Service

In the context of Africa's journey to empowerment, the provision of Basic Public Services is even more critical. The continent has faced centuries of colonization and exploitation, which have left many countries struggling to meet the basic needs of their populations. In order to break free from the cycle of poverty and dependency, African nations must prioritize self-sufficiency and self-reliance in all aspects of development.

Providing essential services such as housing, clean water, electricity, cell phone service internet service, free government emails, free government social media, free Postal Service, and education is crucial for the well-being and development of any society. These basic public services are the building blocks of a functioning and healthy community, and they play a vital role in ensuring that all individuals have the opportunity to live a dignified and fulfilling life.

Where self-sufficiency is crucial in the realm of telecommunications. In today's digital age, access to cell phone service, internet connectivity, and other forms of communication is essential for participating in the global economy and accessing information and resources. By investing in telecommunications infrastructure and acquiring satellites from friendly countries, African nations can ensure that they have the capacity to provide these services to their populations independently.

When it comes to providing Basic Public Services, rural communities often face significant challenges. These areas are typically the most underserved when it comes to infrastructure and essential services, making it difficult for residents to access healthcare, education, and other necessities. However, agricultural parks offer a unique opportunity to address these issues while also promoting economic development and self-sufficiency.

By investing in the infrastructure of agricultural parks, governments can create hubs of activity that provide not only food security and support for local farmers but also access to essential services for rural communities. This includes housing for workers, clean water sources, electricity, and communication services such as cell phones and internet connectivity. By ensuring that these services are available in rural areas, governments can help to bridge the gap between urban and rural development and create more equitable opportunities for all citizens.

Furthermore, the concept of "hybrid governmental partially like Amazon" postal services is a revolutionary idea that can further enhance the provision of Basic Public Services in Africa. By modernizing and streamlining the postal service to operate more efficiently and effectively, governments can ensure that citizens have access to reliable and affordable mail delivery services, both locally and internationally. This can have a significant impact on economic growth and development by facilitating trade, communication, and connectivity between different regions and countries.

Education is another crucial component of Basic Public Services that must be prioritized in Africa's journey to empowerment. By investing in quality education for all citizens, governments can ensure that future generations are equipped with the skills and knowledge they need to succeed in a rapidly changing world. This includes providing free government emails and social media accounts to students, as well as access to online resources and educational materials through the internet.

Basic Public Service: Housing, Health Care, Clean Water, Electricity, Cell Phone Service, Internet Service, free government emails, free government social media, trash management and recycling, free Postal Service "hybrid governmental partially like Amazon" local and international, and Education. For countries that can afford it in Africa, they can buy First Gen Satellites, Second Gen Satellites, or Third Gen Satellites from other friendly countries to support your independent telecommunications services. The words never again must hold a deadly meaning to anyone wanting to use us, bringing harm to our families, or our country ever again, this includes those of our own kind.

In conclusion, the provision of Basic Public Services is essential for the development and well-being of any society, and it plays a crucial role in Africa's journey to empowerment. By prioritizing self-sufficiency and independence in telecommunications services, investing in agricultural parks and rural infrastructure, and modernizing postal services, African nations can create a foundation for sustainable growth and prosperity. With a focus on self-reliance and self-sustainability, Africa has the potential to overcome its challenges and emerge as a powerful and resilient continent on the global stage.

Chapter 7: The Elephant In The Room

In Post-Colonial Africa, The Elephant Looms Large, Unspoken Trut Of Power And Past, Silent Voices Heard At Last, United In Our Qu For Change, For Our Children's Sake We End This Game, Tearing Down The Barriers Of Grief We Cried, So That The Unheard Voice Will Never Die, We Speak Our Truth To Stop The Lies.

he Urgency of Implementing Age Limits for African Leaders

In the quest for a brighter future for Africa, it is imperative that we address the issue of age limits for African leaders. The continent has been plagued by leaders who have held onto power for decades, becoming increasingly disconnected from the reality of their people's lives and needs. This lack of understanding and empathy has led to a slew of detrimental effects on the African population, from economic exploitation to social unrest.

One of the most troubling aspects of having leaders who are out of touch their citizens is the tendency to prioritize their own interests or those of external powers over the welfare of the people they are supposed to serve. History is rife with examples of African leaders who have allowed foreign entities to exploit their countries' resources, leading to immense poverty and suffering for their citizens.

This cycle of exploitation can only be broken by ushering in a new generation of leaders who are more aligned with the aspirations and needs of the African people. It is time for African leaders to stand up for their fellow leaders by advocating for age limits that will ensure a turnover of power and fresh perspectives. Implementing age limits is not about discriminating against older leaders, but rather ensuring that the leadership of a country remains dynamic and in touch with the changing times.

Younger leaders are often more attuned to the needs of their populations, more open to innovation and change, and more willing to work towards a brighter future for all. To facilitate this transition to a new generation of leaders, African countries must take bold steps towards modernization and self-sufficiency.

Here are ten actionable strategies that African nations can implement to propel themselves into a new era of prosperity:

1. Invest in technological advancement to spur economic growth and innovation.
2. Prioritize social development programs to uplift marginalized communities and reduce inequality.
3. Strengthen military capabilities to defend against external threats and ensure national security.
4. Implement sustainable environmental policies to combat climate change and protect natural resources.
5. Encourage entrepreneurship and small business development to boost local economies.
6. Invest in education and skills training to empower the youth and prepare them for the future job market.
7. Promote good governance and transparency to build trust between leaders and their citizens.
8. Foster regional cooperation and integration to harness collective strength and resources.
9. Combat corruption and ensure accountability among public officials.
10. Empower women and marginalized groups to participate in leadership roles and contribute to national development.

By embracing change and implementing age limits for African leaders, we can pave the way for a brighter future for the continent. It is time for African leaders to stand up for each other and prioritize the needs of their people above all else. Together, we can build a prosperous, sustainable, and inclusive Africa for generations to come.

African Coups

Africa has a tumultuous history of coups and political instability, with the continent witnessing numerous overthrows of leaders through violent means. These coups have had a significant impact on the political landscape of Africa, shaping the way leaders come to power and the way governance is conducted.

One of the key discussions surrounding this issue is the role of democracy in African politics, and how it has influenced the continent's trajectory. Thomas Sankara, and Ibrahim Traore are considered heroes to millions in Africa as well as millions in the diaspora for standing up against the powers of colonialism. Is democracy the only way for Africa to go when democracy has condoned assassinations around the world of African leaders, along with democracy being the author of foreign creation.

The idea of democracy in Africa has been a contentious one, with many leaders using it as a facade to maintain power while suppressing dissent. Leaders like Thomas Sankara of Burkina Faso have been seen as examples of figures who sought to bring about democratic reforms in their countries, only to face violent ends through military coups.

Sankara, known as the "African Che Guevara," implemented progressive policies aimed at uplifting the poor and marginalized in Burkina Faso, but was tragically assassinated in a coup orchestrated by his close friend Blaise Compaore. Thomas Sikora is considered to be one of the greatest leaders among others in African history.

These cases highlight the complexities of supporting leaders in Africa, as even those who appear to be championing democratic values can fall victim to the machinations of power-hungry individuals. The Sahel region, encompassing countries like Niger, Mali, and Burkina Faso, has been particularly susceptible to political instability and military coups, with leaders often being toppled by the very military officers they once trusted. Foreign intervention in African politics has also played a significant role in shaping the continent's governance. Western powers have often supported leaders who align with their interests, regardless of their commitment to democratic values.

This has led to numerous authoritarian regimes receiving backing from foreign governments, perpetuating the cycle of corruption and oppression in many African countries. The consequences of such intervention can be devastating, as seen in cases like the Rwandan genocide where Western support for the Hutu-led government exacerbated ethnic tensions and led to the mass slaughter of Tutsis. Labeling governments as democratic without actually upholding democratic principles has also been a common tactic used by many African leaders to legitimize their rule.

This has led to a situation where autocrats masquerade as democrats, using the trappings of democracy to maintain their grip on power while suppressing dissent and stifling opposition. The concept of leadership in Africa is a complex one, with traditional notions of kingship and authoritarianism often conflicting with modern ideas of democratic governance. The debate between traditional kingship and democratic governance in Africa highlights the tensions between preserving cultural heritage and embracing progressive values.

From Colonization to Superpower: Africa's Journey to the Top

Many African countries have a long history of traditional monarchies and chieftaincies, where leaders are chosen based on hereditary lines and hold absolute power over their subjects. While some argue that traditional leaders can provide stability and continuity in government, others contend that democratic governance is essential for ensuring accountability and transparency in leadership.

In order for African nations to navigate towards true independence and develop leaders who prioritize the well-being of their people, a paradigm shift is needed in the continent's political landscape. Leaders must be held accountable for their actions and governance must be transparent and inclusive of all voices. African countries must also prioritize economic development and social welfare, investing in infrastructure, healthcare, and education to uplift their populations and ensure a brighter future for the continent as a whole.

One example of a leader who has sought to prioritize the well-being of his people is Ibrahim Traore of Burkina Faso, who has made significant strides in improving human rights, combating corruption, and promoting economic development in his country. Traore commitment to democratic values and good governance has earned him praise both domestically and internationally, demonstrating that leadership in Africa can be successful when rooted in the principles of accountability and transparency.

In conclusion, the impact of coups in Africa and the role of democracy in the continent's political landscape are complex issues that require careful consideration and analysis. African nations must navigate towards true independence and develop leaders who prioritize the well-being of their people, while also balancing traditional notions of kingship with modern ideas of democratic governance. By learning from the mistakes of the past and embracing progressive values, Africa can forge a brighter future for itself and its people.

African & Diaspora Land Settlements Laws

All African countries should adopt land laws to protect themselves of foreigners, coming in and taking over, by buying large plots of land, rather it's for business or personal use.

Implementing regulations to protect African countries from foreign exploitation and preserve their sovereignty is crucial for the sustainable development and economic prosperity of these nations. Land settlements laws play a significant role in ensuring fair distribution of resources, preventing land grabbing, and empowering local communities.

The only two groups that should be allowed to buy land in Africa is the diaspora and native Africans. African leaders should look at some countries that have good land laws such as the Philippines

Drawing parallels with successful land laws in countries like the Philippines, African nations can learn from the provisions and restrictions that have been put in place to safeguard national interests. For instance, in the Philippines, foreign ownership of land is restricted, and partnerships with local residents are required for land acquisition.

This ensures that the land remains in the hands of the people and prevents large-scale foreign ownership

In the Philippines, you can't buy land unless someone from that country goes on the title as a partner for personal land use, or business use. There should also be land lease laws for private landowners with foreign companies, with no more than a 20-year option before approval and renewal. Foreigners should not be allowed to buy a condo unless 60% of the building is sold to local residence first. This is to protect the diaspora and native Africans not to become like South Africa. The Philippine laws will probably work the best for African countries rights to maintain land sovereignty.

Chapter 8: The Shift in Global Power Dynamics

ion's roar in a distant ancient land, saying come my hildren we have a plan, eagles clash in skies above, the vicked one's gazing showing no love, silent whispers of hange as come, a new world rising from the dust of the riginal one's.

Africa's Growing Influence in International Relations

Africa's growing influence in international relations is a topic that has gained significant attention in recent years. As the continent continues to develop economically and politically, its role on the global stage is becoming more pronounced. From being a region that was once dominated by colonial powers to becoming a key player in international affairs, Africa's journey to the top has been a remarkable one.

One of the key factors driving Africa's growing influence in international relations is its economic growth. With a growing middle class and a rapidly expanding consumer market, African countries are increasingly seen as important players in the global economy. This has led to a rise in foreign investment in the continent, as well as an increase in trade and diplomatic relations with other countries.

Another factor contributing to Africa's rising influence is its political stability. Many African countries have made significant progress in terms of governance and democracy in recent years, leading to more stable and predictable political environments.

This has made the continent a more attractive partner for other countries looking to engage in international relations.

addition, economic and political factors, Africa's growing influence in international lationships can also be seen and its cultural impact. Africa music, art, and fashion are creasingly becoming popular around the world, helping to shape the global trends and rception of the continent this culture influence is helping to raise African profile on the ternational stage and attract more attention from other countries.

verall, Africa's growing influence in international relations is a positive development for e continent and for the world as a whole. As African countries continue to develop and pand their influence, they are playing an increasingly important role in shaping global affairs. is presents new opportunities for collaboration and partnership and has the potential to bring out positive change on a global scale.

The Decline of America and Europe

As we delve into the topic of the decline of America and Europe, it is important to acknowledge the historical context that has led us to this point. Both continents have long been seen as superpowers, dominating global politics, economics, and culture. However, in recent years, we have witnessed a significant shift in power dynamics, with Africa emerging as the next superpower on the world stage.

One of the key factors contributing to the decline of America and Europe is the rise of nationalism and populism in both continents. This has led to increased polarization, social unrest, and a weakening of democratic institutions. As a result, these once-powerful nations are struggling to maintain their influence and relevance in a rapidly changing world.

Another major factor in the decline of America and Europe is the economic challenges they are facing. Both continents have been hit hard by the global financial crisis, leading to widespread unemployment, poverty, and social inequality. This has eroded the social fabric of these societies and weakened their ability to compete on the world stage.

Furthermore, the rise of China and other emerging economies has further challenged the dominance of America and Europe. These countries have been able to leverage their economic power to expand their influence globally, while America and Europe have struggled to adapt to this new reality. As a result, their power and influence have waned, paving the way for Africa to rise as the next superpower.

In recent years, Africa has been making significant strides towards achieving the status of a global superpower. With its rapidly growing economy, expanding influence on the world stage, and increasing political stability, the continent is poised to emerge as a major player in the international arena. This shift in power dynamics has the potential to reshape the global order and challenge the dominance of traditional superpowers like the United States and Europe.

In conclusion, the decline of America and Europe is a complex and multifaceted phenomenon that is reshaping the global power dynamics. As Africa emerges as the next superpower, it is crucial for us to understand the underlying factors driving this shift and to prepare for the opportunities and challenges that lie ahead. By recognizing these trends and working together to build a more inclusive and sustainable world, we can ensure a brighter future for all.

Emerging Superpower Status for Africa

One of the key factors driving Africa's rise to superpower status is its economic growth. With a young and rapidly growing population, abundant natural resources, and increasing foreign investment, many African countries have experienced impressive rates of economic expansion in recent years. This economic growth has enabled African nations to invest in infrastructure, education, and healthcare, laying the foundation for long-term development and prosperity.

In addition to its economic strength, Africa's increasing diplomatic influence and political stability have also contributed to its emergence as a superpower. The continent has played a key role in mediating conflicts, promoting peace and security, and advocating for the interests of developing countries on the world stage. African leaders have also been at the forefront of initiatives to address global challenges such as climate change, poverty, and inequality, further enhancing the continent's reputation as a rising global power.

As Africa continues to assert itself as a major player in international affairs, it is also positioning itself as a leader in the digital age. With a rapidly expanding tech sector, a growing number of online influencers, and a large and engaged online audience, Africa has the potential to shape the future of the digital economy and influence global trends in technology, entertainment, and social media. This digital revolution is not only driving economic growth and innovation but also empowering African voices and amplifying the continent's influence on the world stage.

As we witness Africa's journey towards superpower status, it is important for Blacks, politicos, and online influencers to recognize the continent's potential and support its continued growth and development. By fostering partnerships, promoting investment, and amplifying African voices and perspectives, we can help ensure that Africa's rise to superpower status is not only successful but also sustainable and inclusive. As Africa emerges as a global powerhouse, we have the opportunity to celebrate its achievements, learn from its successes, and work together towards a more prosperous and equitable world for all.

Chapter 9: Challenges and Opportunities for Africa's Rise

Amidst chaos and strife, Africa stands tall, her people resilient, refusing to fall. Sparkling eyes reflect delayed dreams, but their spi remain unswayed. Through turmoil and pain, they fight for their rig with courage and hope shining brightly. From darkness to light, the strive to ascend, building a future that knows no end.

Political Stability and Governance

Political stability and effective governance are crucial components in Africa's journey to becoming the next superpower. Without these key elements, the continent will continue to struggle with social unrest, economic instability, and lack of progress. In order for Africa to rise to the top, it must first address the issues of corruption, weak institutions, and ineffective leadership that have plagued many countries in the region. region.

One of the main challenges facing Africa is the prevalence of corruption within its political systems. Corruption not only undermines the rule of law and erodes trust in government institutions, but it also hinders economic growth and development.

In order to combat corruption, African countries must implement strong anti- corruption measures, hold corrupt socials accountable, and promote transparency and accountability in government operations.

Weak institutions are another obstacle to political stability and effective governance in Africa. Many countries on the continent lack the capacity to deliver basic services, enforce laws, and protect the rights of their citizens. Strengthening institutions such as the judiciary, law enforcement agencies, and civil service is essential for building a stable and effective government that can address the needs of its people and promote development.

Effective leadership is also critical to achieving political stability and good governance in Africa. Leaders must be committed to serving the interests of the people, upholding the rule of law, and promoting transparency and accountability in government operations. By electing leaders who are dedicated to the welfare of their citizens and the development of their countries, Africa can create a more stable and prosperous future for its people.

In conclusion, political stability and effective governance are essential for Africa to realize its full potential and become the next superpower. By addressing the issues of corruption, weak institutions, and ineffective leadership, African countries can build strong and stable governments that serve the interests of their people and promote economic development. With the right policies and leadership in place, Africa has the potential to rise to the top and lead the world into a new era of prosperity and progress.

In the quest for Africa to rise as the next superpower, socio-economic development and poverty alleviation play crucial roles. Historically, colonization has left a lasting impact on the continent, leading to widespread poverty and economic disparities. However, with strategic policies and initiatives, Africa has the potential to overcome these challenges and emerge as a global leader in the 21st century.

One of the key strategies for socio-economic development in Africa is the empowerment of black communities. By investing in education, healthcare, and entrepreneurship within these communities, African countries can create a more inclusive and equitable society. This not only reduces poverty but also fosters a sense of pride and unity among the people, driving overall progress and development.

Socio-Economic Development and Poverty Alleviation

Political leaders in Africa play a critical role in driving socio-economic development and poverty alleviation. By implementing policies that promote economic growth, job creation, and social welfare, and education these leaders can create a conducive environment for businesses to thrive and for individuals to uplift themselves out of poverty. Moreover, by addressing issues of corruption and mismanagement, political leaders can ensure that resources are allocated effectively and efficiently, benefiting the entire population.

Online influencers also play a significant role in shaping the narrative around Africa's journey to becoming a superpower. By sharing success stories, promoting investment opportunities, and highlighting the continent's rich cultural heritage, online influencers can inspire a new generation of African leaders and entrepreneurs. Through their platforms, they can amplify the voices of marginalized communities and advocate for policies that promote social justice and equality.

As Africa rises as the next superpower, the fall of America and Europe is not a foregone conclusion. Instead, it presents an opportunity for collaboration and partnership between continents. By leveraging each other's strengths and resources, Africa, America, and Europe can work together to address global challenges such as climate change, poverty, and inequality. Through mutual respect and cooperation, these continents can create a more sustainable and prosperous future for all.

Harnessing the Potential of African Youth

the sub-chapter "Harnessing the Potential of African Youth," we delve into the critical role that the ıth in Africa play in the continent's journey to becoming a superpower. African youth are the future ders, innovators, and change-makers of the continent, and it is essential that we harness their tential to drive Africa's growth and development.

e of the key strengths of African youth is their creativity and ingenuity. With the right support and ources, African youth have the potential to come up with innovative solutions to the continent's llenges, whether it be in the fields of technology, agriculture, healthcare, or education. It is crucial that we vide them with the necessary tools and opportunities to unleash their creativity and drive positive nges in their communities.

ucation is another key factor in harnessing the potential of African youth. Investing in quality education all young people in Africa is essential for equipping them with the skills and knowledge they need to ceed in the modern world. By ensuring that all African youth have access to a quality education, we can power them to reach their full potential and contribute to the continent's growth and development.

ntorship and support from experienced professionals and leaders are also crucial in nessing the potential of African youth. By providing mentorship and guidance to young ple, we can help them navigate the challenges they face and develop the skills and fidence they need to succeed. It is important for established leaders in Africa to take an ve role in mentoring the next generation of leaders and providing them with the support y need to thrive.

harnessing the potential of African youth is essential for the continent to reach its full ential and become a superpower. By investing in their creativity, education, and ntorship, we can empower African youth to drive positive change and lead Africa to righter future. It is time for all stakeholders, including governments, businesses, and civil iety, to come together and support the youth in Africa on their journey to success.

CHAPTER 10: THE ROLE OF BLACK LEADERS AND ONLINE INFLUENCERS

Black leaders, loud and clear voices, online Influencers,

Speaking hope is near. society shaped, change inspired,

advocates for justice, empowerment required.

Mobilizing the African Diaspora for Development

In today's global landscape, the African diaspora plays a crucial role in the development and progression of the continent. As individuals who have roots in Africa but now reside in other parts of the world, the diaspora holds immense potential to contribute to Africa's growth and success. Mobilizing the African diaspora for development is essential in harnessing the skills, resources, and knowledge of these individuals to drive positive change on the continent.

One of the keyways to mobilize the African diaspora for development is through fostering a sense of connection and belonging to the continent. Many members of the diaspora may feel disconnected from Africa due to factors such as distance, cultural differences, or lack of opportunities. By creating platforms for engagement, networking, and collaboration, we can empower the diaspora to actively participate in development initiatives and projects that benefit their countries of origin.

Furthermore, governments and organizations must recognize and leverage the unique skills and expertise that the African diaspora possesses. From professionals in fields such as technology, finance, healthcare, and education to artists, entrepreneurs, and activists, the diaspora is a diverse and talented group that can drive innovation and progress in Africa. By providing opportunities for diaspora members to share their knowledge, mentorship, and resources, we can accelerate development efforts and create sustainable impact across the continent.

In addition to individual contributions, collective action and advocacy are essential in mobilizing the African diaspora for development. By uniting under common goals and priorities, diaspora communities can amplify their voices, influence policies, and advocate for change at local, national, and international levels. Through partnerships with governments, non-profit organizations, and businesses, the diaspora can drive initiatives that address key challenges facing Africa, such as poverty, inequality, and environmental degradation.

Ultimately, mobilizing the African diaspora for development is not just a matter of necessity, but a powerful opportunity to harness the potential of a vast and dynamic network of individuals who share a common heritage and vision for Africa's future.

By fostering collaboration, innovation, and solidarity among diaspora members, we can unlock new possibilities for growth, prosperity, and sustainable development on the continent.

It is time for the African diaspora to rise up, unite, and drive Africa's journey to becoming a superpower, alongside the fall of America and Europe.

Empowering the Next Generation of African Leaders

Empowering the Next Generation of African Leaders is crucial in shaping the future of the continent and positioning Africa as the next superpower alongside the fall of America and Europe. As the world continues to shift towards a more globalized and interconnected society, it is imperative that Africa cultivates a new breed of leaders who are not only capable of navigating the complexities of the modern world but also have a deep understanding of the continent's unique challenges and opportunities.

One of the keyways to empower the next generation of African leaders is through education. By investing in quality education that is relevant to the needs of the continent, we can equip young Africans with the skills and knowledge necessary to drive sustainable development and innovation. This includes fostering critical thinking, problem-solving, and leadership skills that will enable them to tackle the pressing issues facing Africa today, from poverty and inequality to climate change and political instability.

Another important aspect of empowering African leaders is providing them with opportunities for mentorship and networking. By connecting young leaders with experienced professionals and policymakers, we can help them gain valuable insights and guidance that will enable them to make informed decisions and navigate the complexities of the political landscape. Additionally, networking can help young leaders build alliances and partnerships that will enable them to collaborate on projects and initiatives that have the potential to drive positive change in Africa.

Moreover, empowering the next generation of African leaders also involves creating platforms for them to amplify their voices and share their ideas with a wider audience. In today's digital age, online influencers play a crucial role in shaping public opinion and driving social change. By engaging with online influencers who are passionate about Africa's development, we can help young African leaders reach a global audience and raise awareness about the continent's potential as the next superpower.

In conclusion, empowering the next generation of African and Diaspora leaders is essential for Africa's journey to the top and the fall of America and Europe. By investing in education, mentorship, networking, and online influence, we can create a

new breed of leaders who are not only capable of driving sustainable development and innovation but also have the vision and determination to transform Africa into a global powerhouse. It is time for Blacks, Politico, and Online Influencers to come together and support the next generation of African leaders in realizing their full potential and shaping the future of the continent.

Chapter 11: The Future of Africa as a Global Superpower

Africa's rising strength, defying chains of past, emerging victorious from shadows cast, through trials and tribulations, blossoming like a flower, a global phenomenon, with limitless power.

Potential Scenarios for Africa's Ascendancy

As the world continues to shift and change, Africa's potential for ascendancy is becoming increasingly evident. In this subchapter, we will explore some potential scenarios for Africa's rise to superpower status and the implications it may have on the global stage. From economic growth to political influence, Africa has the potential to reshape the current world order in ways that have never been seen before.

One potential scenario for Africa's ascendancy is through economic growth and development. With a rapidly growing population and abundant natural resources, Africa has the potential to become a major player in the global economy.

As more African countries embrace technology and innovation, they are positioning themselves to compete with traditional economic powerhouses like the United States and Europe. This economic growth could lead to increased political influence and power on the world stage.

Another potential scenario for Africa's ascendancy is through political alliances and partnerships. African as a continent most start and continue to strengthen their relationships with other black nations, realizing they are building a network of support that could bolster their position as a world superpower. By forming alliances with other countries in Africa and around the world, Africa could leverage its resources and influence to enact change on a global scale. This could lead to a shift in power dynamics that favors African interests over those of traditional Western powers.

One key factor that could contribute to Africa's ascendancy is the fall of America and Europe. As Western powers struggle with internal divisions and economic challenges, Africa has the opportunity to step into the void and assert itself as a new global superpower. By capitalizing on the weaknesses of America and Europe, Africa could position itself as a leader in areas such as technology, trade, and diplomacy. This shift in power dynamics could have far-reaching implications for the global order and pave the way for a new era of African dominance.

Chapter 12: Black Influencers

Drenched in strength and grace, black influencers their words and deeds immortal, their voices loud while seeing, speaking, and exposing lies, cultivating change, inspiring echoes of greatness, shaping minds, hearts, souls forever in heavenly places.

Black News Influencer

For Blacks, Politico, Online Influencers, and those interested in the niche of "Africa The Next Superpower Along With The Fall Of America and Europe," the potential scenarios for Africa's ascendancy offer a glimpse into the future of global politics and economics. By understanding the factors that could contribute to Africa's rise to superpower status, individuals in these niches can better prepare for the changes that lie ahead. From economic growth to political alliances, Africa's journey to the top is poised to reshape the world in ways that have never been seen before. It is up to us to embrace this potential and work towards a future where Africa takes its rightful place as a leader on the world stage.

Black influencers are one of the most important tools for blacks to be heard around the world, and yet not one African country has mobilized this unstoppable, relentless power for their potential advantage.

It may take one Black influencer to unite in solidarity the other Black influencers to come together under one framework, Worldwide Association, or Global Union, and in unity to finance themselves by breaking away from global platforms they do not own, as did Phillip Scott with African Diaspora News Channel app. This innovative and imaginative individual realize the importance of not depending on global platforms he didn't own and started his own autonomous self-owned app, and by doing this he created his own news conglomerate. This supremacy and sovereignty need to occur under black control only to insert a black global presence.

Black influencers have already made a dynamic change in the way news is presented on the worldwide stage today. Their exposing unwanted truths that mainstream media hide purposely in order to deceive and control blacks across the earth with purposeful duplicities of misleading deliberate deceptions of false truths.

We must vigorously support Black influencers not only because they're a conduit for the black perspective, but they're creating an independence self-governing news affiliation being heard all over the planet with a boisterous loud voice for a group of people who had no voice on the world stage.

In conclusion, Like other nationalities lets support our Black Influencers by subscribing and funding your favorite black news influencers channel(s) and become a part of the black news revolution.

Leveraging Social Media for Advocacy and Awareness

In today's digital age, social media has become a powerful tool for advocacy and raising awareness on important issues. For the Black community, leveraging social media platforms can be a game changer in the fight against systemic racism and inequality. By using platforms like Twitter, Facebook, and Instagram, Black activists and organizations can amplify their voices and reach a wider audience than ever before. This has the potential to spark meaningful conversations, educate the public, and mobilize support for important causes.

Politicians can also benefit from utilizing social media for advocacy and awareness. By engaging with their constituents online, politicians can build trust, share important information, and gather feedback on key issues. Social media platforms provide a direct line of communication between politicians and the public, allowing for more transparency and accountability in government. Politicians can use social media to showcase their work, connect with voters, and rally support for policy changes that benefit the Black community and other marginalized groups.

Online influencers play a crucial role in shaping public opinion and driving conversations on social media. By using their platforms to raise awareness about important issues facing the Black community, influencers can inspire their followers to take action and support meaningful causes. Whether it's sharing educational resources, promoting grassroots campaigns, or calling out injustice, online influencers have the power to make a real impact on social media. By leveraging their influence, online influencers can help amplify the voices of Black activists and organizations and bring attention to issues that are often overlooked by mainstream media.

As Africa rises to become the next superpower on the global stage, social media can play a key role in showcasing the continent's progress and achievements. By sharing success stories, promoting African culture and innovation, and highlighting the continent's potential, social media can help change the narrative around Africa and challenge negative stereotypes. Social media can also be used to advocate for policies that benefit African countries, raise awareness about important issues facing the continent, and mobilize support for pan-African initiatives. By harnessing the power of social media, Africans can amplify their voices, connect with the global community, and work towards a brighter future for the continent.

In conclusion, social media has the potential to be a powerful tool for advocacy and awareness in the Black community, among politicians, online influencers, and Africa as the next superpower. By leveraging social media platforms, individuals and organizations can amplify their voices, raise awareness about important issues, and mobilize support for meaningful causes. Whether it's fighting against systemic racism, advocating for policy changes, or promoting Africa's rise on the global stage, social media can be a catalyst for positive change and progress. It's time for Blacks, politicians, online influencers, and Africans to harness the power of social media and work together towards a more just, equitable, and prosperous future.

Chapter 13: Implications for Global Politics and Economics

Destiny, melding strength and wisdom, in an insane world of dreams while shaping the world's future, knowing nothing is what it seems, a beacon of hope in the dawn's coming light, in a reality full of evil, Africa prepares for the fight.

From Colonization to Superpower: Africa's Journey to the Top

In examining the implications for global politics and economics in the context of Africa's rise as the next superpower, it is crucial to understand the historical and contemporary dynamics at play. Africa's journey from colonization to potential superpower status represents a significant shift in the global power structure, with far-reaching consequences for both Africa and the rest of the world.

One key implication of Africa's rise as a superpower is the changing dynamics of global politics. As Africa asserts itself on the world stage, it will inevitably challenge the dominance of traditional global powers such as America and Europe. This shift in power dynamics has the potential to reshape international relations, leading to new alliances, conflicts, and geopolitical strategies. The emergence of Africa as a superpower will require a reevaluation of traditional power structures and a reimagining of global governance systems.

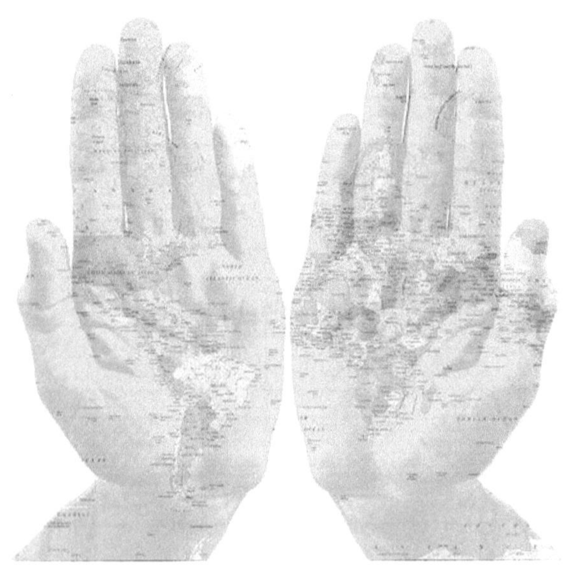

Economically, Africa's rise as a superpower represents a significant opportunity for growth and development. With a young and rapidly growing population, abundant natural resources, and a burgeoning middle class, Africa has the potential to become a major player in the global economy. As Africa's economy continues to grow, it will attract investment, trade, and business opportunities from Diaspora around the world, further solidifying its position as a key player in the global economy.

For Black individuals, politicians, and online influencers, Africa's rise as a superpower presents a unique opportunity to showcase the continent's potential and challenge stereotypes and misconceptions. By highlighting Africa's achievements and contributions to the global community, Black individuals can inspire pride and confidence in their heritage and identity. Politicians can leverage Africa's rise to forge new partnerships and alliances that benefit their constituents, while online influencers can use their platforms to amplify African voices and perspectives on the world stage.

In conclusion, the implications for global politics and economics of Africa's journey to superpower status are vast and multifaceted. As Africa continues to assert itself on the world stage, it will challenge traditional power structures, reshape international relations, and drive economic growth and development. For Black individuals, politicians, and online influencers, Africa's rise presents an opportunity to showcase African excellence, challenge stereotypes, and forge new partnerships that benefit not only Africa but the global community as a whole.

Chapter 14: The Responsibility of Africa as a Superpower

In the heart of the world, Africa transcends, the mighty lion, untamed but wise. With vast lands and ancient souls, he holds power beyond man's control. His roar echoes through valleys and plains, guiding nations, soothing pains of those trodden on, A superpower as in the ancient days he shall be, bringing hope, change, and unity.

The Responsibility of Africa as a Superpower

Africa's rise as a potential superpower in the global arena is not just a possibility, but a responsibility that the continent must embrace. With a rich history, diverse culture,

and abundant resources, Africa has the potential to become a major player on the world stage. As a continent that has long been exploited and marginalized by Western powers, it is time for Africa to take its place as a leader and influencer in the international community.

One of the key responsibilities that Africa must take on as a superpower is to lead by example in promoting democracy, human rights, and good governance. By setting a high standard for these values within its own borders, Africa can show the world that it is capable of governing itself effectively and fairly. This will not only benefit the continent's citizens but also earn Africa respect and credibility on the global stage.

Another crucial responsibility for Africa as a superpower is to address the pressing issues facing the continent, such as poverty, corruption, and conflict. By using its influence and resources to tackle these challenges head-on, Africa can improve the lives of millions of people and create a more stable and prosperous continent. This will not only benefit Africans but also strengthen Africa's position as a global leader.

In addition to addressing internal challenges, Africa must also take on a leadership role in addressing global issues such as climate change, terrorism, and economic inequality. By working with other nations and organizations, Africa can help shape international policies and initiatives that benefit not only the continent but the entire world. This will demonstrate Africa's commitment to being a responsible and proactive global citizen.

As Africa rises to superpower status, it is essential for the continent to remain true to its values, culture, and identity. By staying true to its roots while embracing modernity and progress, Africa can inspire other nations to follow its lead and create a more equitable and just world. Africa's journey to the top is not just about power and influence but about using that power responsibly to make the world a better place for all.

Chapter 15: Conclusion: A New Era of Possibilities and Challenges

From colonial rule to power's embrace, Africa's journey of hope and grace. Resilience blooms through challenges it faced, endless possibilities in this transform state.

Conclusion: A New Era of Possibilities and Challenges

In Africa's journey to the top represents a new era filled with countless possibilities and challenges. The continent has come a long way from being colonized and exploited by foreign powers to now emerging as a potential superpower on the global stage. With its rich resources, diverse cultures, and young population, Africa has the potential to lead the world in various sectors such as technology, innovation, and economic growth.

However, Africa's rise to the top also comes with its own set of challenges. The continent still grapples with issues such as political instability, corruption, and lack of basic infrastructure. In order to fully realize its potential, Africa must address these challenges head-on and work towards building a more stable and prosperous future for its people.

As Black individuals, politicians, and online influencers, it is important for us to support and promote Africa's journey to the top. By highlighting the continent's achievements and potential, we can help shift the global narrative about Africa and inspire others to invest in its future. Africa's success is not only beneficial for the continent itself, but also for the entire Black diaspora around the world.

With Africa on the rise, the possibility of it surpassing America and Europe as a superpower is not far-fetched. As the world continues to evolve and global power dynamics shift, Africa has the opportunity to assert itself as a major player on the world stage. By harnessing its resources, talent, and innovative spirit, Africa can pave the way for a new era of prosperity and progress.

In conclusion, Africa's journey to the top is a testament to the resilience, creativity, and potential of the continent and its people. As we look towards the future, let

us continue to support Africa in its quest for greatness and work towards a world where Africa stands at the forefront of innovation, progress, and success. Africa is indeed the next superpower, and its rise will shape the future of the world for generations to come.

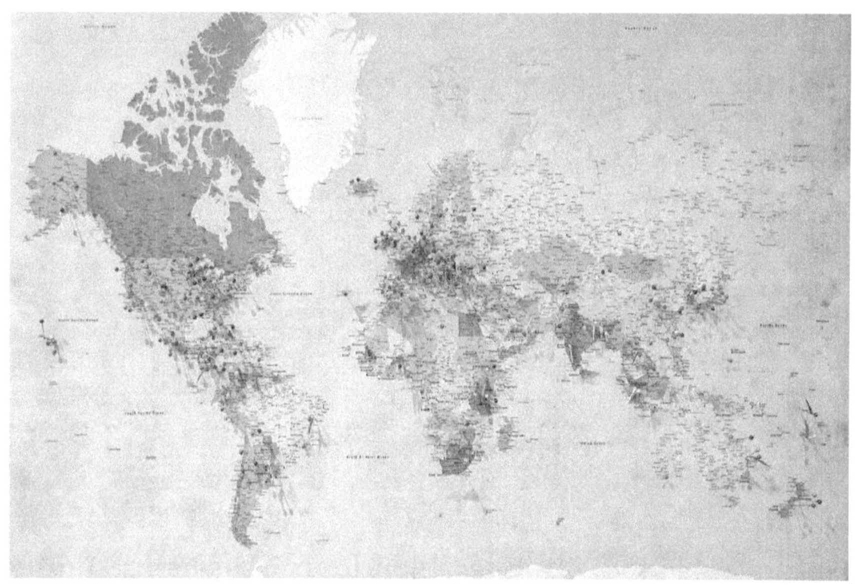

Chapter 16: The Diaspora Global Flags

Flags soar high, colors blend, In diaspora unity w transcend, roots across oceans we ascend, colonization' legacy, we bought to an end, and should another hol uprising ever fall upon us, Yah's men, I give my wor brother I'll fight till we win.

Global Diaspora Flag

This is a 9-star flag, it is to remember our 9th level genetic vibration, with a crown of the true Kings and Queens of the Earth, Green is the land we own, and will own again, yellow is the glory of our God spirit, and black is the melanin of the Creator's people. (Created By Angelo Quentin)

Diaspora Flag Of War

This 18-star flag is to remind us of the 9th vibrational land we were taken from, and the land we were taken to, the crown is of the true Kings and Queens of the Earth, Green is the land they will own again. Yellow is the glory of our God spirit, black is the melanin of the Creator's people. Red is for the blood spilled of our people, and the price that must be paid for that blood. (Created By Angelo Quentin)

Global Black Hebrew Flag

Red represents our blood. Yellow represents our spirit. Green represent our land. Blue represents the water surrounding that land.

Created By Angelo Quentin

From Colonization to Superpower: Africa's Journey to the Top

Attention:

Unlock Africa's Untold Story!

Interest: "From Colonization to Superpower: Africa's Journey to the Top" is not just a book; it's a treasure trove of meticulously researched information and insights. Dive deep into the history and future of Africa with strict copyright and licensing terms ensuring authenticity and credibility.

Desire: Imagine being part of a journey that unveils the resilience and greatness of an entire continent. Readers around the world are raving about this transformative masterpiece as it sheds light on Africa's path to becoming a global superpower.

Action:

Don't miss out on this enlightening experience, get your hands on and reading "From Colonization to Superpower: Africa's Journey to the Top" today!

The Author's Book-Bio

In the book "From Colonization Superpower: Africa's Journey to the Top" by Angelo Quentin, the author provides insight into his motivations for writing the book and offers background information about his African heritage and his desire to educate others about the rich history potential of the continent.

One key point Quentin emphasizes in this chapter is the need to challenge stereotypes and misconceptions about Africa. He aims to highlight the resilience and achievements of African societies throughout history, as well as the continent's potential for growth and development in the future. By sharing his own perspective as an African writer, Quentin hopes to inspire readers to reconsider their perceptions of Africa and engage with its complex history and diverse cultures.

The author's perspective as an African writer undoubtedly influences the overall narrative and themes of the book. Quentin's personal investment in the subject matter is evident in his passionate advocacy for African agency and empowerment. His emphasis on Africa's journey from colonization to superpower reflects a desire to shift the discourse away from a narrative of victimhood and towards one of resilience and progress.

Critiquing the chapter in terms of clarity, relevance, and impact on the reader's understanding, Quentin's author bio effectively establishes his credibility and expertise in the field of African history. By sharing his personal motivations for writing the book, Quentin establishes a connection with readers and invites them to engage with the material on a deeper level.

Overall, "From Colonization to Superpower: Africa's Journey to the Top." Quentin's personal investment in the subject matter adds a layer of authenticity and passion to the narrative, making it a compelling read for those interested in African history and empowerment

www.ingramcontent.com/pod-product-compliance
Lightning Source LLC
LaVergne TN
LVHW040945150826
845672LV00002B/551

9798230512226